GOT THE WHOLE WORLD WATCHING

"An ambitious blend of autobiography and cultural criticism."

—*New York Times Book Review*, **Editors' Choice**

"Wonderful. . . . While *Invisible Man, Got the Whole World Watching* may not have the answers, its attempt to define the undefined something buzzing about blackness feels like catching lightning in a bottle."

—*Atlantic*

"[Mychal Denzel Smith] provides perspective into the complexity of blackness that's commonly lost in discussions about race. . . . This memoir is both groundbreaking and saddening. It might be the first of its kind: a book that offers a comprehensive look into the genesis of black millennial lives through the eyes of a young black man."

—*Chicago Tribune*

"Mychal Denzel Smith has written an engaging and brilliant book about his growth and transformation as a black man in the United States."

—*Truthout*, **Progressive Pick**

"A philosophical work. . . . [Mychal Denzel Smith's] straight-forward explanation of his experience growing up as a black man in America is worth our urgent attention."

—*Minneapolis Star-Tribune*

"What makes *Invisible Man, Got the Whole Watching* so revolutionary is Smith's brutal honesty. . . . Unlike many of his predecessors, [Smith] gives a raw recount of a young black man's life through the framework of black feminism and cultural criticism."

—*National Post*

"Smith's honesty is raw and often funny, and his punches land squarely. . . . Smith will continue to be a voice for our nation in years to come. . . . A commanding read."

—*Library Journal*

"A useful blueprint for radical and intersectional politics in a country where a black child can grow up to be president but where living while black is still dangerous."

—*Kirkus Reviews*

"It has become routine to witness black boys meeting violent ends. Captured on police dash cams or bystander smart phones, we watch black boys die as videos replay hourly on cable news and are clicked feverishly on YouTube. It is still rare to watch black boys grow—to hear them laugh or cry, to declare their passions, and to reason carefully. This is part of why Smith's book is so affirming, necessary, even delightful despite its brutality and angst. Mychal Denzel Smith answers the pressing but unasked question, what would happen if all those black boys felled by bullets had a chance to make mistakes, read books, fall in love, hone skills, take new paths, and grow up? The story is fully and unflinchingly Mychal's, and because Mychal is so distinctively self-aware, so intellectually invested, and emotionally raw, it cannot simply stand in as a generic tale for all the lost black boys—except that they too would have had stories entirely their own to tell if only they had had a chance to write them. We owe it to them and more importantly to ourselves to read Mychal's book and render visible what we would rather forget."

—MELISSA HARRIS-PERRY,
Maya Angelou Presidential Chair, Wake Forest University

"Decades ago, Toni Cade Bambara wrote, 'The purpose of a writer is to make revolution irresistible.' Mychal Denzel Smith, in addition to crafting a genius piece of art that swims through politics and prose, has created one of the first books of my lifetime that makes structural and interpersonal revolution irresistible. Unlike many twentieth- and twenty-first-century memoirs written by black men, Smith convinces readers that any conversation or movement toward black liberation that doesn't also reckon with heteropatriarchy is brittle at best, and likely destructive. *Invisible Man, Got the Whole World Watching* is the first book of my life that I need to read with my mother, my grandmother, and my children. Mychal Denzel Smith has done it. He has written a potential revolution."

—KIESE LAYMON,
author of *How to Slowly Kill Yourself and Others in America*

"It isn't often that a book comes around that is so honest, so reflexive, so self-aware without being either self-aggrandizing or self-effacing, that it makes you literally want to write your own memoir. Mychal Denzel Smith manages to do it all—make us laugh, reminisce, reflect, cry, and testify all at once. *Invisible Man, Got the Whole World Watching* is not your average coming-of-age story. Rooted in the political history of the last thirty years, Smith masterfully describes the shifting connotations of black identity and masculinity in public and private space. Caught in a web of respectability politics, misogyny, and homophobia, not only are the prospects of success for black freedom movements elusive—so are the immediate futures of black communities. *Invisible Man* challenges us to reexamine the origins and the implications of systems of oppression on our families, our communities, our world, and ourselves inside the broken promises of hope and change for Black America."

—ALICIA GARZA,
co-creator, #BlackLivesMatter, and special projects director,
National Domestic Workers Alliance

"*Invisible Man, Got the Whole World Watching* is quintessentially Mychal Denzel Smith: brilliant, honest, courageous, hilarious, and transparent. Most importantly, it is one of the best and most authentic examples of black male feminist cultural criticism that we have ever seen. Although he draws from his own experience, Mychal avoids the self-importance and navel gazing that compromise most memoirs of this genre. Instead, he offers a narrative that is at once unique and ordinary, reflective and instructive. This book should be read by anyone trying to understand what it means to be black and male and committed to this beautiful struggle for freedom."

—MARC LAMONT HILL,
author of *Nobody: Casualties of America's War*
on the *Vulnerable, from Ferguson to Flint and Beyond*

"With this book, Mychal Denzel Smith solidifies his place as one of the most important voices of his generation. A gifted story-teller with sharp political analysis, he straddles the personal and political with aplomb. This is a book everyone should read."

—JESSICA VALENTI,
columnist, *Guardian* (US), and author of *Sex Object: A Memoir*

"Mychal Denzel Smith takes us on a political and cultural journey of young black manhood that unapologetically examines, parallels, and weighs the influence of Obama and LeBron, Kanye and Trayvon, Malcolm X and Chappelle on his own becoming in the twenty-first century. By centering the black boy he once was, the boy many refuse to see, we face him head-on. Smith trusts us to not only see him in all his vulnerability, bravado, and incisiveness, but to know him. This is Smith's selfless offering."

—JANET MOCK,
New York Times **bestselling author of** *Redefining Realness*

"This is the book that black parents should reach for when the time comes for 'the talk'—the difficult conversation with their sons about how to become a man in a minefield of racialized risk. Smith takes up the contested terrain of black masculinity and mines the contradictions of a social world that delivered both a black president and a seemingly endless body count of black lives lost. But Smith offers us more than yet another narrative of black male endangerment. Through poignant, probing, and revealing reflections, Smith takes the reader to places that others won't—to the vexed visions of antiracism that equate racial uplift with heteronormative visions of the family, to the compromised state of black politics, and to a more robust conception of what an intersectional vision of racial justice might look like. This is rich material that others will mine, but none will be as unflinching, as provocative, as insightful as Mychal Denzel Smith."

—KIMBERLÉ WILLIAMS CRENSHAW,
distinguished professor of law, UCLA Law School,
and director, Center for Intersectionality
and Social Policy Studies, Columbia Law School

"If I kept a diary of my deepest thoughts, plaguing insecurities, and varied triumphs—this would be it. It is a cover-to-cover conversation with the reader on the complexity of (hopefully) growing to be a Black Man in the American Empire. Mychal's coming-of-age book, his first, is a masterful meld of personal reflection, political analysis, and honest insight that yearns to be felt, must be read, and demands to be seen."

—UMI SELAH,
organizer and cofounder, the dream defenders

"Mychal Denzel Smith is one of the most important and vibrant voices of his generation. Born into the grim and brutal realities of systemic racism, police violence, and the prison industrial complex, Smith's work—searing yet funny—is, in some ways, a miracle. He has survived the grave challenge of simply being a young black man in America and has lived to tell the tale. Smith's writing, speaking, and television appearances, as well as his incisive use of social media, inspire one to imagine what it would be like if James Baldwin, Richard Wright, or Ralph Ellison were on Twitter."

—JEREMY SCAHILL,
author of *Dirty Wars* and *Blackwater*

INVISIBLE MAN,
GOT THE WHOLE
WORLD WATCHING

INVISIBLE MAN, GOT THE WHOLE WORLD WATCHING

A Young Black Man's Education

MYCHAL DENZEL SMITH

NATION
BOOKS
New York

Nation Books
116 East 16th Street, 8th Floor New York, NY 10003
http://www.publicaffairsbooks.com/nation-books
@NationBooks

Printed in the United States of America

First Trade Paperback Edition: October 2017

Published by Nation Books, an imprint of Perseus Books, LLC, a subsidiary of Hachette Book Group, Inc.
Nation Books is a co-publishing venture of the Nation Institute and the Perseus Books.

The Hachette Speakers Bureau provides a wide range of authors for speaking events. To find out more, go to www.hachettespeakersbureau.com or call (866) 376-6591.

The publisher is not responsible for websites (or their content) that are not owned by the publisher.

"Invisible Man, Got the Whole World Watching" comes from "Hip Hop"
Hip Hop
Words and Music by David Axelrod, Michael T. Axelrod, Mos Def, Joseph Kirkland and Gabriel Jackson
Copyright © 1999 EMI Blackwood Music Inc., Glenwood Music Corp., Medina Sound Music, Empire International Music Inc., Dusty Fingers Music and Street Tuff Tunes
All Rights on Behalf of EMI Blackwood Music Inc., Glenwood Music Corp., Medina Sound Music and Empire International Music Inc. Administered by Sony/ATV Music Publishing LLC, 424 Church Street, Suite 1200, Nashville, TN 37219
International Copyright Secured All Rights Reserved
-contains elements of "The Warnings" and "Spoonin' Rap"
Reprinted by Permission of Hal Leonard Corporation

Print book interior design by Jeff Williams.

Library of Congress Cataloging-in-Publication Data
Names: Smith, Mychal Denzel, 1986- author.
Title: Invisible man, got the whole world watching : a young black man's education / Mychal Denzel Smith.
Description: New York : Nation Books, 2016. | Description based on print version record and CIP data provided by publisher; resource not viewed.
Identifiers: LCCN 2016021355 (print) | LCCN 2016006482 (ebook) | ISBN 9781568585284 (hardcover) | ISBN 9781568585291 (ebook)
Subjects: LCSH: African American young men--Race identity. | African American young men--Social conditions--21st century. | African American young men--Education. | United States--Race relations. | Smith, Mychal Denzel, 1986-
Classification: LCC E185.625 (print) | LCC E185.625 .S635 2016 (ebook) | DDC 305.242/10896073--dc23

ISBN: 978-1-56858-977-0 (paperback)

LSC-C

10   9   8   7   6   5   4   3   2   1

We did it,
Slim

CONTENTS

Introduction

The NBA's Western Conference All-Stars had a sizeable lead over the Eastern Conference All-Stars, 88–69, when George Zimmerman killed Trayvon Martin. It started with a 911 call on the night of February 26, 2012:

This guy looks like he's up to no good, or he's on drugs or something. It's raining and he's just walking around, looking about. . . . He looks black. . . . A dark hoodie, like a grey hoodie, and either jeans or sweatpants and white tennis shoes. . . . He's just staring . . . looking at all the houses. . . . He's got his hand in his waistband. And he's a black male. . . . Something's wrong with him. Yup, he's coming to check me out, he's got something in his hands, I don't know what his deal is. . . . These assholes, they always get away.

Zimmerman followed the suspicious-figure-turned-asshole. The 911 dispatcher told him they didn't need him to do that, so he stopped. Briefly. He then decided he needed a more accurate address in the event the police called him back and he needed to let them know exactly where he was. While he was trying to get that information, the suspicious figure in a hoodie attacked him. The asshole emerged from the bushes, punched him in the face, knocked him to the ground, and pinned him down. He screamed for help. The asshole, who was destined to get away, punched him repeatedly, still pinning him to the ground, while his head bounced off the concrete sidewalk with each blow. Not knowing if he would survive the attack, and with no help forthcoming, he began reaching for his gun. The suspicious figure saw what was happening and started reaching for the gun as well. "You're going to die tonight," the suspicious asshole told Zimmerman. He was left with no other choice. He reached the gun first. He shot the asshole in the chest. "You got me!" the hoodie-clad suspicious asshole said as he fell to his death.

That's the story Zimmerman told. That's the story the Sanford Police Department believed. It's a story as old as America itself. It's a story about black men's inclination toward violence, our reliance on animal instincts, our general unfitness for civilized society, our preference for death and destruction.

To believe this story—where Trayvon was the aggressor, a teenage boy more interested in fighting a stranger than getting back home to see if LeBron James, Derrick Rose, Carmelo Anthony, and Dwyane Wade could lead the Eastern Conference All-Stars in a comeback, that he brought Zimmerman close to death with his bare hands—is to believe the stories white supremacy has always told about black boys and men in America. You don't need to hate black men in order to believe these stories. Black men's humanity only need be invisible to you, so you never question where these stories came from and why they exist.

Far too many people were content to do just that. That's how Zimmerman was able to raise a little over $200,000 for his legal defense fund in less than two weeks, a month before he was even arraigned. The only weapons found on Trayvon's body were the can of Arizona Iced Tea and a bag of Skittles he had just purchased from the local 7-Eleven, but it was Zimmerman, with a gun on his hip, they believed had cause to fear for his life. For those people, Trayvon was everything they ever believed black men to be.

For the rest of us, Trayvon Martin became another of our martyrs. His name became a rallying cry, his Skittles a reminder of lost innocence, his hoodie a symbol of resistance, his family a living memory of what American racism steals from us.

He didn't ask for any of it. Before he was a symbol, he was just a boy. He liked football, and Lil Wayne, and airplanes, and taking things apart to put them back together. He was a black boy in America trying to become a black man. George Zimmerman made him into another black boy that would never have that opportunity.

I don't remember what I was doing when George Zimmerman killed Trayvon Martin. I'm sure I was watching the same All-Stars game, as I had done since I was a kid even younger than Trayvon. I may have even made a snack run to 7-Eleven. I almost certainly was tweeting, or at the very least reading Twitter. I may have been on deadline and convincing myself that watching the game wasn't procrastinating but all a part of my writing process. I was probably stressing about money. I probably wasn't thinking about dead black boys.

I've had the opportunity to do a number of things Trayvon will never have the chance to, and the guilt of that weighs heavily on me. Everything Trayvon did that supposedly justified his death—wear hoodies, walk to the store at night, buy Skittles, have tattoos, smoke weed, be suspended from school—I did. I could have been Trayvon. So many of us black boys trying to become black men in America could have been. Knowing this made his death that much harder to stomach.

One of the more pernicious effects of racism on the psyche is the constant questioning of one's worth and purpose. It can be almost as debilitating as death. Almost. I don't wish to make these things seem equivalent. I have my life; Trayvon does not. But the source of my guilt is understanding that American racism will take some of our lives while holding others of us up as exemplars of success, providing the illusion that there is an escape. It places us in the unenviable position of wishing that our martyrs could have survived to become tokens.

I tried to imagine who Trayvon would have been on February 26, 2013, 2014, 2015, 2016, and beyond. The things he would have seen, the world he would have known, how he would have created himself. When you're introduced to a martyr as a result of their death, they aren't a whole person. They are a name and a story. They are a set of symbols and projections. Their lives are flattened for our consumption, and whatever attempts we make to remind ourselves of their humanity are no substitute for the face-to-face interactions we'll never have with them.

There's a particular pain in that realization when the martyrs are as young as Trayvon. I didn't get to know who Trayvon was, but as a seventeen-year-old he probably hardly knew himself. He liked football, Lil Wayne, airplanes, and taking things apart to put them back together, but he never got the opportunity to ask himself why. He never had his assumptions challenged, never had his worldview shattered, his heroes humanized, or his morals questioned. He never had to confront his own bigotry or his complicity in different systems of oppression. To ask who he would have been on February 26, 2013, 2014, 2015, 2016, and beyond is to try to fill in the gaps where only experience can be the guide, and George Zimmerman took the opportunity for experience away from Trayvon.

Trayvon Martin was a seventeen-year-old black boy in America. White supremacy tells a lot of lies about seventeen-year-old black boys who grow up in America, but we can't escape the fact that those black boys absorb a culture of misogyny, homophobia, transphobia, class-based elitism, self-hatred, violence, untreated mental illness, and a host of other American problems that translate differently when experienced through the lens of American racism.

I don't want to appear to be tarnishing the image of Trayvon Martin, a black boy I never knew. There's an almost instinctual desire to protect our martyrs, so many of them being young black men viciously maligned in life and unable to escape the barbs of racism in death. If we don't rescue their narratives, they'll forever be remembered only to the extent that white supremacy lends them any humanity. But we do a disservice to our martyrs by imposing perfection upon them. We do a greater disservice to ourselves, the survivors and potential tokens, by not honestly reckoning with who our martyrs were and who they could have been.

We resist this conversation because black men and the culture they create so easily become scapegoats. Without nuance, it very quickly turns toward a blaming of black men for the existence of misogyny, homophobia, and the rest of those American problems, not a careful examination of how black men can experience or contribute to these forms of oppression. And the more the image of black men is connected to everything wrong with the world, the easier it is to justify killing us. Racism comes to be seen as a natural reaction to the existence of black monsters.

Who would Trayvon Martin have been on February 26, 2017, 2018, 2019, 2020, and beyond? The short answer: he would have been a black man in America. The long answer involves figuring out exactly what that entails.

I was twenty-five years old when George Zimmerman killed Trayvon Martin. I hadn't prepared for life at twenty-five, having believed at different points of my life that I wouldn't make it that far. I could have been Trayvon, or any number of nameless, faceless black boys killed by police or vigilantes, by other black men, or themselves. Twenty-five was a relief and a surprise and an opportunity. I would be afforded the time to create myself that Trayvon wasn't.

I didn't know how to do that. Or, I didn't know how to do that and become a healthy and whole human being. It seemed that every black man I witnessed attempting to create himself came through to the other side broken. They walked through the culture of misogyny, homophobia, transphobia, class-based elitism, self-hatred, violence, untreated mental illness, and other American problems and emerged as living proof of the lies white supremacy tells about black boys and men in America. I was doing the same, because I knew no other way.

Then George Zimmerman killed Trayvon Martin. I looked at the face of the boy who became a symbol and wanted more. I wanted more for him than the choice between martyr and token. I wanted more for him than eulogies and praise songs. I wanted more for him than just an opportunity to create himself. I wanted for him, for all the Trayvons in waiting, a world where they didn't have to grow up broken or not grow up at all.

I wanted to figure out how to create that world. I looked at my own life and asked how I made it to twenty-five. I asked who influenced me to think the way I did, what events had been most important in shaping my worldview, who and what challenged me to see it all differently. I asked myself: How did you learn to be a black man?

Then I wrote down some answers, for the martyrs and the tokens, for the Trayvons that could have been and are still in waiting.

Chapter 1

My parents sent me to college to become a credit to my race. It was never said in those exact words, but the idea was planted early on that my life would be one where I would defy all of the stereotypes associated with being a black man. I wasn't allowed to sag my pants, or say the "n-word," or listen to rap music that had explicit lyrics. My mother corrected my English whenever I dropped my g's or started a sentence with "me and . . ." I wasn't supposed to ever give anyone the opportunity to think of me as less than. Academic excellence was the biggest part of being "twice as good" and therefore a college education was non-negotiable. It was the key to the future my father envisioned for me. He wanted me to be an upstanding citizen with unimpeachable credentials who could gain everyone's respect so they might see me as more than "just another black man" and come to see me as a man. My parents wanted me to become Barack Obama.

They never said it in those words either, of course, because they didn't know who Barack Obama was. Hardly anyone did until July 27, 2004. He was an Illinois state senator with no national profile. He wrote a memoir that was released in 1995 that had a modest public reception. He ran for Congress in 2000 and lost. But four years later here he was, a candidate for an open U.S. Senate seat and being tapped to deliver the keynote address at the Democratic National Convention.

I didn't see the speech, because I didn't see any of the convention, because I thought electoral politics was inherently corrupt and useless. The first election I ever paid attention to was determined by hanging chads and the Supreme Court, and ultimately gave us George W. Bush as president. I wasn't about to put any faith in that kind of system.

But I heard plenty about Obama's speech the next day. My father was gushing about it. I had never known him to have any strong political opinions. My parents read the newspaper every morning and watched the news every night, but that was the extent of their political dedication. The most they said about politics to me and my little brother was that voting was important. But now, after hearing Obama speak, suddenly my father was a pundit. He was so impressed, he wished Obama were the one running to defeat Bush's reelection campaign instead of the settled-for John Kerry. Obama was everything Kerry wasn't. Naturally charismatic. A dynamic speaker. Youthful. Relatable. Black.

But the right kind of black. The successful, respectable kind of black. The kind of black that was "twice as good," that made itself known and then faded. The kind of black that would allow people to just see a man. The kind of black man my father was raising me to be.

I was curious enough to want to see what had my father, and everyone else, so excited. It wasn't hard to find out, thanks to 24-hour cable news. All I had to do was turn on CNN and witness Obama on a loop, saying, "There's not a black America and white America and Latino America and Asian America; there's the United States of America."

There was more to the speech, but that was the part that got repeated the most, and I wasn't impressed. Obama seemed to be trying to get the country to forget about racism at precisely the same time I was ready to raise the most hell about it. He was emerging as the kind of figure I had been taught to admire, but I did everything to reject the moment I started seeing the world differently.

I was born in 1986 in Washington, D.C., when Ronald Reagan was presiding over the early phase of the War on Drugs. I grew up the son of a career Navy man in Virginia Beach, Virginia, during the 1990s, while Bill Clinton triangulated politics, exploded the prison population, and slashed welfare. I entered high school the year of George W. Bush and purged voter rolls. A conservative America was the only America I had ever known, and before 9/11 I didn't think to question it. I was the son of a Navy man who had served under Republicans and Democrats and never uttered a single negative word about either in my presence. He was proud to serve his country and carry out his missions no matter who was commander in chief. My mother always made sure I was reading black authors and learning black history, but that didn't carry over into a formalized ideology. I didn't seek out any political education on my own, and living inside the bubble of American-born ignorance suited me just fine.

But after the towers fell and Bush took the country to war in Iraq, the apolitical stance I'd adopted became insufficient to help me process what was happening in the world. I was unclear about where to turn to make sense of it all. Until I found *The Boondocks*.

The first time I saw Aaron McGruder's comic strip *The Boondocks* was in the July 1998 issue of *The Source* magazine with Master P on the cover. I couldn't actually listen to any Master P records in my house, but my mother always supported reading, so I talked her into letting me get a copy of *The Source*. And there, after reading about the LL Cool J–Canibus beef, I saw Huey, Riley, and Caesar being everything my parents raised me not to be. They weren't corny like the characters in *Jump Start* and *Curtis*, the only two black comic strips in my local newspaper.

But the Internet is magic, and when my cousin, Marcus, showed me that not only did *The Boondocks* exist in the form of two book collections but could also be seen daily on Okayplayer.com, it was as if the blackness messiah had come down to lay hands on me personally. I found it just as McGruder and the strip were hitting their anti-Bush-administration stride, calling them out for lying about weapons of mass destruction and the ways in which the U.S. government had previously supported Saddam Hussein. But at the same time, McGruder was also skewering contemporary hip-hop culture, criticizing the crass materialism and obsession with gangster culture. And while the daily strip was explaining current events, reading the collections introduced me to part of the canon of black consciousness—Huey P. Newton, Frantz Fanon, Public Enemy, and Malcolm X.

I'd known Malcolm for most of my life. There was one piece of art I can remember hanging on the wall wherever we lived. It was really simple—a drawing of the heads of three major Civil Rights–era figures, something you might find from a street vendor or at an African or African-American themed festival in your town. Ours was of Martin Luther King Jr., the Honorable Elijah Muhammad, and Malcolm X. Malcolm was in the center; his head was the largest.

One of my fondest early memories is of a Black History Month program that my father participated in while we were living in Naples, Italy. It was the Navy's way of recognizing that, indeed, Black History Month was a thing and there are black people in our ranks. They had different service men and women dress the parts of notable black historical figures and then deliver speeches in character. I was four years old, and I watched the program from a theater balcony as my father, already kind of looking the part, stood and delivered as Malcolm X.

Then, in second grade, I chose to do my Black History Month project on Malcolm X. We were tasked with turning shoe boxes and paper towel rolls into a kind of movie reel that would have images and words about an important black historical figure. My mother took me to the library to check out all the (age-appropriate) books I could about him. My father let me borrow some of his books, too, including his copy of *The Autobiography of Malcolm X*. I didn't understand much of what I read, but I knew the words excited me. I knew Malcolm excited me. He meant something special to me even before I could articulate what that something was.

Malcolm X excited me because he was dangerous. I knew that much because when I gave the presentation of my project, several of my white classmates started crying and my teacher made me stop before I finished. It was about three or four of them, one right after the other, their faces turning bright red with only their tears to interrupt the discoloration, upset as I told them about how Malcolm X believed in fighting "the white man" by any means necessary and he brandished the guns to prove it.

I remembered this episode when, at sixteen, I reread *The Autobiography of Malcolm X*. I was actually able to understand it this time, and I was better able to say what it was about Malcolm that filled me with pride. He was a student first, devouring every bit of knowledge that he could, and a teacher second, imparting his hard-earned wisdom to a people rejected from formal schooling. His uncompromising truth-telling made white people uncomfortable, so much so that whenever I brought him up in my history classes, my teachers quickly pivoted to Martin Luther King Jr. and non-violence and dreams and color-blindness. I knew Malcolm was a threat—my second-grade classmates' tears taught me that—but when I finally came to understand why, I held the threat close. The threat represented a truth I had, to that point, failed to see. Malcolm taught us that white supremacy was the enemy of self-love. He preached pride in our blackness as both a birthright and a tactic against an American system of devaluation. And he was killed for it.

I liked the idea of being that powerful and hated the idea of being defined by America's racism. There had to be more to being black than the slavery and KKK I learned about in second grade, or that kid calling me a nigger in sixth grade, or a teacher advising me not to speak Ebonics in the eleventh grade, or my parents telling me to be "twice as good" all of my life. Malcolm X, as I knew him, was the perfect amalgamation of black genius and confidence needed to resist the system. He was my most important teacher, but following his example meant seeking more. I wasn't going to find them at school because we had only ever been assigned two black authors and learned about the Civil Rights movement in half of a single class period. And I wasn't going to find them at home, because we had taken down the Elijah/Malcolm/Martin portrait and never replaced it.

The teachers most readily available to me, who followed Malcolm's model, came from hip-hop. My parents may have been able to regulate my listening choices when I was ten, but at sixteen I had the Internet and cashiers who didn't check my ID at the CD counter. I was free to consume all the curse-word-laden gangsta rap my ears could handle.

It was never just the gangsta shit that captivated me, though it did speak to a certain sense of rebellion that lived dormant underneath my shy, reserved persona. But as the wars raged on and the massive assault on civil liberties took root, politics was becoming more central to my life and I wanted music to reflect that. Hip-hop's history gave me Public Enemy, Ice Cube, and KRS-One, the truth-tellers of their time following in the tradition of Malcolm. They were just as uncompromising and unflinching in their critiques of American racism, with the added bonus of some hard-ass beats accompanying them.

Hip-hop's present was giving me the "conscious" rappers—dead prez, Common, The Roots, Talib Kweli, and Mos Def. They would balk at the label ascribed to them, but their music was a portal to a certain type of consciousness that didn't get the most airplay. They were the best rebuttal against the claim that hip-hop was all about guns, drugs, money, jewelry, cars, and sex. Mos Def emerged as my favorite of the bunch, with his heavy Brooklyn accent dripping off his hyperliterate rhymes. Listening to his album *Black on Both Sides* was like a religious experience for me. He was talking about the theft of black culture, corporate greed, racial double standards, the oppression of a police state, addiction, practical street survival tactics, and self-worth. There wasn't another hip-hop album that felt like it was handcrafted with me in mind.

In between the generations represented by Public Enemy and Mos Def was Tupac. He was killed when I was ten years old and was the first celebrity whose death I had any feelings about. I was sad and confused, because I was truly convinced that Tupac was invincible. He was the ultimate outlaw figure of my childhood, representing everything my parents wanted to keep from me—tattoos and guns and thug life. A total disregard for authority and figures representing authority. But I knew Tupac had resonance beyond pissing off my parents and Dan Quayle. When I reengaged with his music at seventeen years old, his legend was wrapped up in so much mythology, it was near impossible to untangle the facts from the myth. He was the son of a Black Panther, started the East Coast–West Coast rap beef, beat up the Hughes brothers, survived five gunshots, faked his own death, and was chilling in Cuba waiting to return like Christ. He was the hip-hop generation's Robert Johnson or Jimi Hendrix—a figure whose life and death were shrouded in mystery, and because of that his musical and cultural influence became inescapable. But Tupac was also a political figure, articulating the rage of a generation that took to the streets in rebellion (called riots by the rest of the world) because the police could beat Rodney King within an inch of his life and be acquitted of all charges brought against them.

In 1994, he told MTV, "We asked ten years ago. We was asking with the Panthers. We was asking with them, you know, with the Civil Rights movement, we was asking. Now those people that were asking, they're all dead or in jail, so what do you think we're gonna do? Ask?"

I wasn't impressed by Barack Obama because he wasn't Tupac. He wasn't Mos Def or Aaron McGruder. He wasn't Malcolm X. Barack Obama was my parent's idea of black excellence: "well" dressed, "well" spoken, advanced degrees from prestigious universities, successful professional, ambitious, nonthreatening, a rebuke to the stereotypes. Twice as good. But he was a politician, and politicians didn't tell the truth. My heroes were truth-tellers, the people who exposed racism and were committed to fighting in the name of black liberation. They knew there was no sense in asking for freedom. Barack Obama, and the speech that made him famous, seemed to be about denying the need for the fight. He wasn't even asking—he was accepting.

I wrote him off because he didn't see what I was starting to see. I was going to college to learn how to avoid becoming who I thought he was—someone whose ambition would have them avoid the truth. I wanted to learn how to be the next Malcolm X, or Frederick Douglass, or W.E.B. Du Bois.

I arrived on Hampton University's campus in August 2004 so I could become a Black Leader. Hampton was the only school I applied to, partly because it fit the most important criteria of being a historically black university, but also because I was lazy and loathed doing paperwork. I promised myself to be more disciplined and vigilant in pursuit of the actual revolution.

I showed up expecting there to be a whole army of people like me. I expected to engage thousands of other young black budding intellectuals about the politics of racism, and how we might unite and organize to bring down the system, with our struggle-weary professors guiding and cheering us along. Instead I found thousands of mini-Obamas and an administration happy to indulge their delusions.

That's not a totally fair description, but at seventeen that's what I saw and I wanted no part of it. I told myself that was the reason I didn't socialize much, that no one there understood me or shared my interests. It could have been true, but I also didn't give them much of a chance. I'd written them off as apathetic and self-absorbed, as the 85 percent that the Five Percenters, a Nation of Islam offshoot, believed were deaf, dumb, and blind. I didn't think they knew Malcolm, or knew Mos Def, and therefore wouldn't know me. So I put my headphones on and tuned them out.

I would win everyone over in class, I thought. I would sit in the back, slouched down and inconspicuous, waiting until the perfect moment to coolly raise my hand and deliver the perfectly worded answer to the question everyone else had tried their hand at but failed to resolve. Everyone would be so blown away, and eager to hear more, that they would let me lead them to the revolution.

That's how it happened in my head every single time, and not once in real life.

First-year classes at Hampton University weren't structured around my desire to showcase my superior intellect. They were mostly general education courses where professors lectured for fifty minutes with either an intense passion for the subject matter or a roving disinterest meant to convey the message "it's in the damn syllabus." With the notable exception of freshman English.

I was ten minutes late the first day of my English 101 class. In every orientation at Hampton, they stressed this saying: to be early is to be on time, to be on time is to be late, and to be late is unacceptable. I wish I could say I was making some grand rebellious statement to institutional conformity, but since being born at 11:20 p.m. after three earlier trips to the hospital, I've generally been late to everything, and English 101 at 6 p.m. on a Wednesday was no different.

I strolled into class around 6:15 with my uniform on—headphones around my ears, backpack secure over my shoulders—and took the first available seat, right next to the door, as if all was normal. Professor Foster stopped midsentence when I walked in, his eyes following me, his grin widening with every second, every step I took. "And got the nerve to have a Malcolm X T-shirt on at that," he finally said, breaking into half-genuine, half-performative laughter.

Professor Foster, who at the time was still finishing up his dissertation and would quickly reply with the date of his graduation to correct anyone who called him "Dr. Foster," was a six-foot-tall, bald black man from Chicago who often ate applesauce on wheat bread as a postclass dinner. I know this because I spent many days in his office after class, not always by choice. In the beginning, to be honest, never by choice. But Professor Foster was an educator—rigorous and engaged—and he saw me. He clocked me from the moment I opened the door.

After noting my Malcolm X T-shirt, Professor Foster skipped ahead in his classroom introduction to show us the place in the syllabus where it talked about tardiness. "If you're more than ten minutes late don't even bother coming. The door will be locked," he told us. The first day was an exception, but there would be no more.

I didn't have to go to his office that day, but I did have to stay after class and listen to Professor Foster sardonically refer to me as Mr. Smith, while asking why I was late, to which I didn't have a good answer, and telling me how much fun he was going to have with me that semester. I hadn't really been challenged, he told me, but that was going to change.

Professor Foster's approach to teaching English 101 was unorthodox. Whenever someone says something in education is "unorthodox," it conjures images of a movie trailer about a nice white lady who goes to the inner city and teaches black youth that rap and poetry are really the same thing. But the norm is so staid that "unorthodox" as descriptor fits. It was "unorthodox" for us to engage with texts created by black authors. It was "unorthodox" for us to engage those texts not just for form, style, and prose but also content. It was "unorthodox" for us to be asked to relate the content to our current political moment. It was "unorthodox" for us to be expected to engage in classroom discussions about ideas where we would disagree with one another while the instructor refused to dictate but rather pushed us to think outside of our own experiences and perspectives. That should be a standard education. We call it "unorthodox."

It was the second or third week of class when Professor Foster opened up by asking us, "Should selling drugs be legal?" There weren't any reading assignments just yet because he was waiting for the add/drop period to end, so class was this freewheeling discussion of whatever struck him that day. Our conversation proceeded at precisely the level anyone would expect from a group of eighteen-year-old college students unfamiliar with drug policy and the history of drug criminalization. Lots of "what's the big deal?" and "weed should be legal" and "just weed, everything else is going too far" and a few "drugs destroy the community" thrown in for faux pro-black effect.

For the entirety of the conversation, I sat waiting for my star-making moment. I was turning over an answer in my head, reworking and rewording it to perfection, to showcase my awe-inspiring brilliance. I waited and waited, but my classmates were an excitable bunch, and Professor Foster encouraged them when disagreement arose, and my reserved demeanor didn't meld naturally into the flow of dialogue. But Professor Foster wasn't going to allow me to stew in my discomfort and apprehension, not I of the Malcolm X

T-shirt and ten-minute tardiness who had, by his estimation, never been truly challenged. "Mr. Smith," he said through that goofy grin, interrupting the excitement, "your thoughts?"

My moment arrived and the pressure was on. I slouched down a bit in my seat, backpack still on and headphones around my neck because I was trying desperately to make that my look, waited a couple beats, and said, "I think selling drugs should be legal."

"Okayyyyyy . . . why?" Professor Foster didn't care that I'd retreated into my shyness. He was going to make me translate the thoughts that bounced around in my head. I still didn't have the wording quite right, but I was on the spot and he wasn't going to let up, so I let it out. "We sell stuff that's harmful to people all the time. Bleach can kill you, fast food can kill you, so why not let people sell drugs? It's the most American form of business aside from prostitution."

I thought that shit was the most clever thing ever uttered. Professor Foster seemed to be the only one even slightly amused or impressed by my observation. My analogy was imperfect, and the quip about prostitution probably distracted a few prudes from my overall point, but my intent stands up—there is a certain kind of moralizing around the drug business that doesn't exist elsewhere, and the criminalizing of certain products and services that are integral parts of American identity, whether we admit it or not, requires an advanced degree in hypocrisy and cognitive dissonance. The advantage of a decade worth of hindsight allows me to better articulate my idea, and maybe if I had worded it that way at the time my classmates would have responded differently. As it was, no one followed me to the revolution.

But Professor Foster did continue to take an interest in me. He made me stay after class for a few moments that day just to say, "You forgot war." He got it, and that made me feel better, though I still felt like I missed an opportunity to gain my classmates understanding and/or adoration.

He kept me after class again not too long after that, this time with the intention of giving me an assignment. An extra assignment. Something not in the syllabus. An assignment that wouldn't be graded but that he expected me to complete nonetheless. These were the perks of having someone take an interest in your education and development.

He gave me a book, one he'd clearly read a number of times given the tattered pages, highlighted passages, and copious notes written in the margins. He wanted me to read it and be prepared to discuss it with him the next week. I don't remember the name of this book. I remember the title had something to do with politics and power, but not much else. I don't remember because I didn't read this book. I started to read it, but halfway through the first chapter I found the heady academic jargon too much of a chore to wade through for required-non-required reading. And while it dealt with race to some extent, it wasn't the kind of "SAY IT LOUD, I'M BLACK AND I'M PROUD" literature that got me excited in those days. But Professor Foster was expecting me to read it, so I skimmed a few other chapters and decided I could fake my way through at least ten minutes of conversation.

"So, what did you think?"

"It was interesting."

"Interesting means you didn't read it."

Professor Foster saw me. He always saw me and I was always left wondering how.

"No, I did. It was interesting. I had never thought about things that way before. There's the stuff about how race affects politics in a way white people don't have to think about. It was interesting."

Professor Foster took his index finger and jabbed it into my shoulder, and he said, "And what about for you? As a man?"

Here was the challenge.

"Ummm, yeah, that too. I had never really considered it that way."

He had mercy on me and let me go, mostly because he had papers to read (our first of the semester), but he knew I hadn't read that book and he wasn't going to let me forget.

I had deliberately skimmed over the stuff about gender and power because I was not at all interested. Then Professor Foster jabbed me in the shoulder.

I needed to take an honest accounting of who I had been reading and listening to, who was shaping my thinking: Malcolm X, Aaron McGruder, Tupac, W.E.B. Du Bois, Mos Def, The Roots, dead prez, Public Enemy, Frederick Douglass, Huey Newton. Or, in other words: man,

man, man, man, man, men, men, men, man, man. And it had never once occurred to me that might be a problem. I would have needed to be conscious of it in order to consider that possibility.

To my newly forming black radical mind, women—more specifically, black women—had a way of existing without being present. It's a natural result of consuming history and culture through the fables of masculine triumph. The centuries-long battle against American racism had been handed to me inside the framework of black male defiance. Douglass's bravery, Du Bois's genius, Malcolm's eloquence, Tupac's rage. The heroic women existed largely in service of ending racist oppression of the men (Ida B. Wells's research on lynching) or as a catalyst for a man's ascendance to greatness (Rosa Parks resting her weary bones so Martin Luther King Jr. could end segregation). And having been raised in the 1990s, where the main concern of racial discourse was the "endangered black man," I had no reason to question the narrative.

And I was never encouraged to question my heroes. Without a second thought, I'd excitedly highlighted passages in Malcolm X's autobiography like, "No *sane* black man really wants integration! No *sane* white man really wants integration! No sane black man really believes that the white man ever will give the black man anything more than token integration. No! The Honorable Elijah Muhammad teaches that for the black man in America the only solution is complete *separation* from the white man!" Malcolm offered the solution to the problem faced by "the black man."

And what of "the black woman"?

"*Beautiful* black woman! The Honorable Elijah Muhammad teaches us that the black man is going around saying he wants respect; well the black man never will get anybody's respect until he first learns to respect his own women! The black man needs *today* to stand up and throw off the weaknesses imposed upon him by the slavemaster white man! The black man needs to start today to shelter and protect and *respect* his black women!"

The solution for black women was the protection of black men, to be looked after as if they were prized possessions, rather than as living, breathing humans with thoughts and ideas of their own. A generous reading would attribute these thoughts to Elijah Muhammad, not Malcolm, while also noting that part of what caused the rift between Malcolm and the Nation of Islam was Muhammad's treatment of the women members. But Malcolm's rhetoric around "the black man" didn't change much after the split, and the notion of black men serving as protectors of black women gave little thought to whether black women could or should exercise autonomy over their own lives.

My more contemporary teachers weren't much better. Mos Def's *Black on Both Sides* was critical to my development, but not once did I question why his screed against racial profiling, "Mr. Nigga," only addressed the issue from the perspective of black men who experience discrimination and prejudice, while the only track to explicitly explore interactions with women was called "Ms. Fat Booty." And

Tupac, for all the praise he receives for his progressive gender views, left us with some of the most fucked-up ideas about women that, as an impressionable seventeen-year-old, I ate up as if there were no other wisdom in the world. In "Brenda's Got a Baby," his much-lauded ode to teenage motherhood, he starts the song, "I hear Brenda's got a baby / but Brenda's barely got a brain / a damn shame / the girl can hardly spell her name." While it's bad enough he begins with Brenda's perceived stupidity, what follows isn't even a story about a foolish young girl making unwise choices. Instead, it's a story of abuse, neglect, poverty, addiction, and a lack of choices at every turn. Were we supposed to believe that Brenda was stupid because she allowed her cousin to molest her? Or because her family exploited her for a welfare check? Or because she chose to support herself through drug dealing and sex work when she couldn't turn to anyone else? What made Brenda so dumb? Tupac never made that clear, and while it seems we're supposed to have some sympathy for Brenda and her situation, it doesn't appear that we were intended to see her predicament as anything but the result of her own diminished intelligence.

Tupac also gave me an introduction to the differentiation between "bitches" and "women." It's the rationale he used to explain how he could produce a song like "I Get Around"—a fun party track that revels in the hedonism that accompanies "loose" women—and "Keep Ya Head Up"—a genuine expression of solidarity with the struggles facing black women, especially those living in poverty. The latter, according to

Tupac, were real women, deserving of our adoration and undying love. The former were bitches, and there's nothing wrong with calling a bitch a bitch.

But even if you allow for the rationale of "calling a thing a thing" to stand, how could men, the oppressive group, claim any legitimacy in defining "bitches," a term used to describe the oppressed? It would only ever be a means of justifying sexist constructions of women's identity. And this is all before you get into the allegations brought against Tupac for sexual assault.

But your heroes aren't to be questioned because it makes the creation of your own mythology that much easier. If you've only ever learned from right-thinking individuals, your own thinking must also always be right. Their shortcomings, then, would become your own, and no one wants to bear the weight of those shortcomings, least of all when your life has been defined through perceived deficiency.

These black men were my guides through the minefield of identity when faced with racism. I was attracted to the bravado, to the reclamation of black excellence. I wanted to absorb their performance of black arrogance as a corrective to self-loathing. But what I hadn't considered was how that ego was gendered. I spent my childhood passively absorbing white supremacist ideas of my invisibility, then unconsciously shrinking myself from the world. Everything I read, listened to, and learned validated my right to existence as a black man in America. But that wasn't the whole equation. Everything I read, listened to, and learned validated my right to existence as a black man in America, but only within the confines of a patriarchal definition of masculine identity. What went unquestioned were the ways my newfound sense of black manhood contributed to the ongoing marginalization of my mother, her twin sister, my grandmother, my high school guidance counselor, and more than half the student population on Hampton University's campus. I began to see myself, but only by refusing to see black women.

The centrality of the black male experience in the discourse of racist oppression has been passed down from generation to generation, through our politics and our culture, and the sad part of this story is that I likely would have never confronted that history if weren't for a bald black man from Chicago jabbing his finger into my shoulder.

It would still take me several months before I would read the autobiographies of Angela Davis and Assata Shakur, before introducing myself to bell hooks, before making Nikki Giovanni and Sonia Sanchez and Toni Morrison part of my intellectual universe. It would be longer still before I did any serious interrogation of how my thoughts and my actions played a role in the maintenance of sexism—or before I even named it sexism. But Professor Foster had set out to challenge me, and he did.

That was a recurring theme of my first semester at Hampton. I was challenged to speak my mind, challenged to see perspectives not my own, challenged to define my politics, challenged to engage my peers, challenged to think better of them, challenged to think better of myself. And that was just what was happening on campus. On the national stage, Barack Obama was steadily gaining notoriety and daring me not to look at him.

For the politically engaged and liberal-leaning on campus, Obama's 2004 Senate win was the only bright spot of election night. George Bush had won—fair and square this time, though Ohio's voting irregularities were conjuring memories we would rather have buried—and for his second term he only promised to fight Iraqis overseas and gay people here at home. But the buzz was all about Obama, our shiniest Great Black Hope to date. That's who everyone really wanted to be president.

I remained ambivalent—about electoral politics generally, and Obama specifically—but hearing Malcolm say "the ballot or the bullet" a few times on repeat left me wondering if my wholesale dismissal of the role of elected officials wasn't a bit hurried. I didn't think Malcolm would want me getting behind Obama, the man who denied that Black America existed, but Obama would prove inescapable.

For Christmas that year, I was given a copy of *Dreams from My Father*, as I suspect many black boys of a certain age were. The parents/parental figures/mentors/role models in young black men's lives are always looking for ways to inspire us to greatness, to get us to understand exactly what it takes to be twice as good, and show us what's waiting on the other side. Obama's 1995 memoir was the latest tool in the "save black boys" arsenal, having risen to the level of modern American classic after the speech.

I wasn't in the business of turning away books, but I also wasn't going to make reading *Dreams* a priority. I did skip to the back and finally read the speech he delivered at the convention in full, since the text was included as an afterword in the 2004 version of the book. On the page, the speech didn't carry any of the electricity that captivated millions and did nothing to convince me I ought to read the memoir. It sat among my other books, Obama's yearning front cover photo peeking up at me from time to time, and my will to ignore it only grew stronger.

My first year at college ended with me losing my modest scholarship for failure to maintain a 3.3 GPA, falling short of my parent's desires and expectations. I always struggled to stay focused on school work, but even more so at that time, when all I wanted to do was plan the revolution and had decided that Professor Foster's class was the only one helping me do that. I had also only made two friends that first year. I returned from summer vacation determined to be more social, open to the idea that my judgments could have been slightly off. Part of this agenda included becoming active in campus organizations. I joined the school newspaper (technically, I joined during my first year, but I only wrote one article and quit when it took too long for them to consider giving me my own column) and the political science club. The former I joined because I liked to write, the latter because I was a political science major and I had a crush on Sharita, the club's president. I'm not as ashamed of this as I probably should be.

She was one of those politically engaged and liberal-leaning people for whom electoral politics was the holy grail. Her goal was to one day be a senator. Her first step toward that was losing the election for freshman class president the previous year, then bringing to life the defunct political science club as its president, while also working on Tim Kaine's 2005 gubernatorial campaign in our shared home state of Virginia. I wasn't totally on board with her politics, but I really liked her smile, and ambition was proving to be more attractive than I once thought.

One of her big events for the political science club, tied in with her job on Kaine's campaign, was bringing the members to a campaign rally happening in nearby Norfolk. Disillusioned as I was with the entire political system, I didn't even know there was an election happening until the opportunity arose to attend this rally taking place in a high school gymnasium. While the main thing driving my even faint interest in going was the thought that I could impress a girl, it just so happened that stumping for Kaine was none other than the nation's only African-American senator, the Great Black Hope himself, Barack Obama. His inescapability was starting to get annoying.

I brought along my barely read copy of *Dreams*, thinking Sharita would find it impressive that I owned a book that hundreds of thousands of other people also owned. I nodded and smiled while discussing the disappointment of 2004 and how important it was to elect Democrats, all the while thinking to myself, "Please just like me already! This is way too painful and I can't pretend much longer." Then Obama was handed the microphone. A few hundred people were standing around, while a lot of the elderly sat on the wooden bleachers of the gym. But everyone was navigating the tension between wanting to give the man their undivided attention and wanting to burst forth with unencumbered joy at being in his presence.

When he started speaking, I finally started understanding. Hope is a muddy concept, but one that can foster innovation. Despite a Hobbesian belief that life is naturally "nasty, brutish, and short," we strive to create the best versions of ourselves because there exists an indistinct possibility that we, through will and creativity, can alter that reality. But we need something, or someone, to help us believe that the effort will be worthwhile. Long before he turned it into a hokey presidential campaign slogan, Obama simply inspired hope.

During a politically volatile time, Obama offered reassurance. He represented a path forward, an escape from a morose and divisive view of the world. He was America's reprieve. And sitting there with those bursting people hanging on his every word, I could see that very clearly. Obama was nimble, exemplifying what would become his trademark balance. He was realistic about the big political fights facing the country, but optimistic about the ability of Americans to set aside their differences to solve our problems. He flexed his intellect without speaking down to people. He found the sweet spot between affable and standoffish, making his audience feel connected without giving too much of himself. His appeal wasn't political. I don't remember a single policy proposal he advocated for in that gym, and that didn't matter one bit. Maybe it should have, but it didn't.

What mattered was Obama seeing his audience and them seeing themselves in him. Norfolk has a large black population, over 40 percent of the city, and the southeast region of Virginia is home to two historically black colleges, Hampton and Norfolk State University. Looking around the gym that day, you would have been forgiven the assumption that every black person within a five-mile radius was in attendance. In what would become another of his trademarks, Obama spoke to the black people in the room without alienating the white people. He colored his speech with decidedly black colloquialisms in between anecdotes about how to get "cousin Pookie" out to the polls. His command of the stage suggested that he didn't just study Bill Clinton but also Def Comedy Jam. His cadence rose and fell like Sunday morning.

He was a black man. He was not, however, a race man. It's hard to be the former and not be seen as the latter, unless you're a Republican. He did not focus his condemnation on the United States' history of racial terror, did not seek explicit redress for the exploitation of black people's labor and creativity. Obama wasn't Dr. King, but he reminded people of Dr. King. He reminded people of their fathers, of Chris Rock, of their pastor, of Denzel Washington, of their storytelling uncle, of Michael Jordan, of the cousin that made it out the 'hood. He was familiar enough to earn admiration and tentative trust.

But as impressed as I was by what I felt from him that day, I couldn't fully embrace him. My cynicism ran deep enough that it couldn't be undercut by pretty speech and symbolic blackness. I was finally intrigued enough, though, to pick up my neglected copy of *Dreams from My Father*. What I read bored me. I didn't think it was horrible, but I had also just read Assata Shakur's autobiography over the summer, and Obama's story and ideology were bland and bankrupt in comparison. But I only needed one highlighted passage to consider that maybe he saw me: "Only Malcolm X's autobiography seemed to offer something different. His repeated acts of self-creation spoke to me; the blunt poetry of his words, his unadorned insistence on respect, promised a new and uncompromising order, martial in its discipline, forged through sheer force of will."

It didn't make a lot of sense to me that someone who found solace in Malcolm would later lend credence to America's racial amnesia, as Obama would do in his convention speech. But there was something there. Malcolm was in his DNA—perhaps not the same way he was in mine, but he was there. For a brief time, I considered that there was a Barack Obama I couldn't see, one perhaps purposefully hidden from view, for fear of the costs of visibility. A lot of us did. A lot of us gave into the hope.

Chapter 2

I bought a copy of Angela Davis's autobiography with money I earned working at Walmart. These are the types of contradictions you have to get used to when your politics don't match the world in which you live.

It was the summer of 2005 and I had just finished my first year at Hampton. Professor Foster taught me that I didn't know anything, and I decided I was going to return in the fall having learned everything. I had four months, which seemed plenty of time. I would spend my days reading the classic books, listening to the classic albums, watching the classic films. At least, when I wasn't stocking produce at Walmart.

It was important to my parents that I have a summer job. After my father retired from the Navy, he settled into a fairly secure position as a car salesman. My mother, who'd spent most of my life up to that point as a homemaker, had been back to work for about five years. With only two kids, myself and my younger brother, we were, by most conventional measurements, a pretty solidly middle-class family. I didn't have to work for basic survival, and while school was in session my father didn't want me to have a job, so I could focus on being twice as good in school. There was also no way he was going to raise someone who didn't understand the value of hard work as he understood it. So, I spent that summer at Walmart.

Which was awful. I liked having my own money, nearly every cent of which went into buying the books and CDs I needed to feed the intellectual curiosity sparked by my first year at college, but earning it meant spending nine hours a day, five days a week moving around crates and pallets of semifresh fruits and vegetables sold for always low prices. I hated it, not only because it ran counter to my laziness, but because it took so much time and energy away from my personal studies. I spent my time after work napping from exhaustion, eating dinner, then going to bed early in the hopes of getting enough rest to make it through the next day. I spent my off days, when I could have been reading and lounging about, doing my required household chores. To sit still with a book was a luxury.

Still, with what little time I had, and thanks also to a nonexistent social life, I read quite a bit. I figured, like my parents, that education was the ticket to avoiding a life of labor similar to my summer job. That's one of the reasons they insisted on me working at Walmart. It was like "Scared Straight" for a middle-class college student. James Baldwin and Assata Shakur became sweet relief.

My father saw me bring home a copy of Angela Davis's autobiography and somewhat jokingly asked, "You not up in that room becoming a radical, are you?" I half-smiled and shrugged, not comfortable enough to lie and tell him no, but too uncertain of what his response would be to say yes. My political consciousness didn't seem like it would fit into his expectations for my twice as good life.

But it wasn't just the books I was reading that were pushing my radicalization. The war in Iraq was two years old, while the one in Afghanistan was closing in on four years, and the U.S. electorate had recently chosen to reappoint George Bush as president, because there is nothing more American than confidently doubling down on a mistake. But the longer the conflict wore on, the higher the death count rose, and the more incompetent Bush and company were revealed to be, the more the opposition to the war grew.

Among black people, the opposition was even more pronounced, according to an NPR report from October 2005, with nine out ten black Americans standing against the war. The opposition was having an effect on the armed forces' recruitment efforts. Black people were overrepresented in every branch of the military, with the exception of the Marine Corps. The Army in particular had relied on large numbers of black people enlisting in order to meet recruitment goals; in 2000, nearly a quarter of new recruits had been African-Americans. But in 2005, according to a *Washington Post* article from March of that year, that number fell to less than 14 percent. In April 2005, the Army missed its recruiting goal by 42 percent. At the same time, the Marine Corps had missed its recruiting goal for four straight months, which was the first time that had happened in a decade.

The military had come to rely on the economically disadvantaged to see enlistment as their salvation. My father served twenty years in the Navy because the options for him as an eighteen-year-old high school graduate who had grown up poor in southeast Washington, D.C., were basically nonexistent. While things weren't drastically better in 2005, pursuing a nonmilitary job certainly held more appeal to young black men than prolonged deployment in a war with no end in sight.

The military reacted by trying to sweeten the deal, increasing signing bonuses and college scholarships for new recruits. They also hit the recruiting pavement hard. In Virginia Beach, a military town if there ever was one, the sight of men and women in uniform was nothing new to me. We bought groceries and Christmas trees and saw the doctor and went to the beach on base. I was surrounded by uniforms. What was new was that men and women in uniform were now approaching me in the mall, the bank, or Barnes & Noble to tell me all the things a career in the military could offer. Not just once or twice, but on a near weekly basis. What was new was that recruiters started calling our house, and I was politely dismissing their faux sincerity. What was new was my understanding that they targeted young black men for recruitment, and were doing so knowing they would be sending us overseas to kill.

Summer is watermelon season. Walmart sells everything in bulk, and watermelons were no exception. I spent all of July moving, lifting, and hating watermelons—the only time in my life I defied this particular stereotype. Toward the end of the month, I wore the hate and exhaustion on my face.

On one especially cruel day, I took my afternoon break alongside two of my coworkers, something I never did, because I was thirsty for commiseration. We sat on a bench just outside the building, the two of them lighting up cigarettes, when three men approached us. On break, we were not obligated to answer any customer questions, and in all of my irritation I was planning to ignore them.

"What's up, fellas?"

My coworkers, more relaxed than I, responded with pleasantries.

"Any of you guys ever thought about joining the Marines?"

I stewed in my silence. My coworkers told them no, but the three recruiters, dressed in plainclothes and doing their best "yo, I'm just like you" voices, pressed me.

"What about you?"

"No, and I never will."

"Why is that?"

"I have a problem with authority. I don't like being told what to do."

"See, that's why you need the military, it'll teach you some discipline. It'll give you structure."

"I don't want any."

"I can see you won't get very far with that attitude."

"Tell your fucking president that if he got the fuck out of Iraq you motherfuckers wouldn't be having such a hard fucking time recruiting people, that way you could leave me the fuck alone."

"That's okay, it's clear you don't have the character to be in the Marines."

"Good. I'm tired of you motherfuckers calling my house, coming up to me on the street because you motherfuckers can't meet your recruiting goals."

"One, you're going to stop calling us motherfuckers. . . ."

"Mother. Fucker. I said leave me alone."

"Yeah, you don't have the mental toughness needed."

"Right. If you give me a gun, I'll shoot people on my side. On purpose."

"Haha, I'm a trained Marine, who do you think is going to win between me and you?"

"The gun."

Our fifteen minutes was coming to an end, and I was more angry than when it started. Adrenaline had every inch of my skin buzzing. I walked away with my hands balled into fists, prepared to protect myself, but in that state more likely to start a fight. My coworkers laughed like I was performing a routine. The Marines had insulted my character and intelligence in the service of empire. And they were black. In the moment, I couldn't think of any sin greater.

It was a delicate time. "Support our troops" was an effective right-wing talking point, positioning anyone who was antiwar as anti-troops. In polls, the military is consistently the most trusted institution in America, and the men and women who serve are revered as heroic for the simple fact of their service. Whenever I would get my hair cut down low, people would ask if I served and I would have to deal with their disappointed faces when I told them no, robbing them of the opportunity to thank me for protecting them. Here, I'd spent ten minutes cursing out a few Marines, finding myself further on the fringes.

But I had reached my breaking point. My thoughts weren't just on their insults, or my irritation for having been approached by recruiters all summer, or the injustice of the war, or my shit Walmart job. I thought of all those things, and the fact that in the moment these three approached me, the options for young black men in America were laid bare. Cog or killer.

My parents told me I could be whatever I wanted. I just had to work hard, get my education, and then work hard. But as we signed up for loans to pay for an education we couldn't actually afford, I thought about how crippling the pursuit of higher education can be when there's no guarantee that it will lead to the expanded opportunities that American folklore promises. Some of us take the risk. For others, it's cog or killer.

Walking away from those Marines, feeling their eyes looking through the back of me, I felt an anger that was wholly new to me. The irony is that I went back to work more productive than before, burning off the energy produced by my rage. For the next few days, those ten minutes sitting on the bench were all I could think of. The mix of pride and embarrassment and regret (you always think of the best one-liners once the moment is over) mingled with my anger, but it was never enough to overtake it. In the words of Howard Beale, I was mad as hell.

But even if I had decided I wasn't going to take it anymore, what was "it" and how would I resist? I had cursed out three Marines out of two million active duty members of the armed forces who have no decision-making power. I had anger, a year's worth of college education, and a growing book collection purchased with money earned moving watermelons for one of the world's biggest corporations. I had, essentially, nothing.

Experiencing this anger in solitude created a sense of loneliness that only produced more anger. From what I could see, no one else was mad as hell about what was happening to young black men. It wasn't that no one knew. My parents knew, that's why they sent me off to school. Professor Foster knew, that's why he jabbed his finger in my shoulder. My classmates knew, that's why they did everything to avoid talking about it. But I wanted to talk about it. And not just talk about it, I wanted to do something about it. The individual act of cursing out a representative of the system wasn't enough. I wanted more action and I wanted more people on my side, but there was nothing to spark the fire.

Until Kanye said, "George Bush doesn't care about black people."

I may not have known all that I thought I knew when I got to campus in August 2004, but I did know every single word of Kanye West's *The College Dropout* album (only now am I considering the implications of that). Kanye had been my favorite hip-hop producer for a few years, since Jay Z dropped *The Blueprint*, so the occasion of him releasing his own album was my own personal holiday. I kept it in rotation for the better part of a year because, to my fairly uninitiated ears, it was one of the most original and creative things I'd ever heard. Kanye was also the first rapper whose in-rhyme biography I could relate to while still enjoying the music. The projects that produced Jay Z and Nas, the shootouts that produced 50 Cent and Game, the hustling that produced T.I. and Clipse, the dirty south that produced Outkast, the pimping that produced Snoop Dogg, and the white boy angst that produced Eminem didn't reflect my suburban buppie-aspirant upbringing. And while my socially/politically conscious heroes—Mos Def, Talib Kweli, Common, The Roots—stirred my rebellious mind, helping me make sense of the world and how it saw me, they rarely pushed me to look inward, to see myself. Kanye was able to locate the space in the middle of all of that, where sped-up soul samples, ego tripping, self-reflection, and indictments of racism coexisted in harmony, all from an ostensibly middle-class black perspective, while desperately seeking 'hood acceptance.

But Kanye, being Kanye, was starting to garner the most attention for the ego part of the equation. The man has never been shy about voicing his opinions, and he put the world on notice when, after walking out of the 2004 American Music Awards, he told reporters: "I felt like I was definitely robbed, and I refuse to give any politically correct bullshit-ass comment . . . I was the best new artist this year." Just a few months later he put on an all-white suit and went on stage to accept the Grammy Award for Best Rap Album and said, "I know . . . I know everybody ask me that question, they want to know, 'What Kanye is getting well louder, he's gonna do something crazy.' Everybody want to know what I would do if I didn't win. . . . *I guess we'll never know.*"

For some, this was unearned cockiness and immaturity. To me, it was the perfect, unabashed celebration of his black genius self—and by extension, my black genius self. Kanye took over the airwaves in the summer of 2005, and his raps about gold diggers and diamonds from Sierra Leone were helping to keep me sane while pushing apples and bananas to Walmart's sales floor at 7 a.m. Several delays in the release of his next album were unwelcome, but I knew the final product would be worth the wait.

Late Registration was released the day after Hurricane Katrina began destroying New Orleans.

More than 1,800 people dead. A million-plus displaced from their homes. Levees broken. Eighty percent of New Orleans underwater. Over a hundred billion dollars in damage. "The single most catastrophic natural disaster in U.S. history." George Bush flying overhead. "Brownie, you're doing a heckuva job."

The numbers and gaffes don't tell the whole story. Black people were turned into refugees in their home country and we all watched it happen. We tuned into CNN for days and weeks to see images of mostly poor black people asking for someone, anyone, to come save their lives. The bodies of the dead discarded. The bodies of the hopeless screaming out in agony. The white flags being waved at helicopters from the roofs of drowned-out homes. The children bathed in excrement and desperation. The water refusing to recede. The New Orleans heat offering no relief. The United States government offering even less.

In 1997, President Bill Clinton announced his "One America in the 21st Century: The President's Initiative on Race," which was intended "to promote a national dialogue on controversial issues surrounding race." Since then, whenever a news story hints toward the possibility of the existence of racial discrimination, our collective reaction has been to call for the convening of a "national conversation on race." Around the time I was preparing myself for a job as a Black Leader, that national conversation on race tended to revolve around questions as vital as: Is affirmative action still needed? Is affirmative action reverse discrimination? Who is and isn't allowed to say the n-word? What influence is gangster rap having on our children? Why do smart black kids get teased for "acting white"? Is Tiger Woods black? Is Tiger

Woods being teased for acting white while listening to gangster rap and reverse discriminating by benefiting from affirmative action?

Hurricane Katrina was the first instance, in my lifetime, where our national conversation on race had to concern itself with questions of inequality, poverty, and government neglect. It provided a visual representation of what I understood intellectually—years of divestment, legal discrimination, and inattention to the plight of black Americans had led to a crisis. And it was infuriating to witness.

On September 1, 2005, New Orleans Mayor Ray Nagin gave voice to that fury in an interview with a local radio station:

> I am very frustrated because we are not able to marshal resources and we're outmanned in just about every respect. . . .
>
> And they don't have a clue what's going on down here. They flew down here one time two days after the doggone event was over with TV cameras, AP reporters, all kind of goddamn—excuse my French everybody in America, but I am pissed. . . .
>
> I'm like, "You got to be kidding me. This is a national disaster. Get every doggone Greyhound bus line in the country and get their asses moving to New Orleans." . . .
>
> And I'll tell you, man, I'm probably going get in a whole bunch of trouble. I'm probably going to get in so

much trouble it ain't even funny. You probably won't even want to deal with me after this interview is over. . . .

I don't want to see anybody do anymore goddamn press conferences. Put a moratorium on press conferences. Don't do another press conference until the resources are in this city. And then come down to this city and stand with us when there are military trucks and troops that we can't even count. . . .

Don't tell me 40,000 people are coming here. They're not here. It's too doggone late. Now get off your asses and do something, and let's fix the biggest goddamn crisis in the history of this country. . . .

I am just—I'm at the point now where it don't matter. People are dying. They don't have homes. They don't have jobs. The city of New Orleans will never be the same in this time.

Nagin caught his fair share of criticism for not having a plan in place to evacuate the thousands of people in New Orleans who relied on public transportation, or simply didn't have the resources to be able to leave their homes, but in that moment, his expression of rage was transformative. Radio host Garland Robinette, who interviewed the mayor, said in the documentary *When the Levees Broke*, "That was the moment I think we started getting help."

That could have been the end of the story. New Orleans could have gotten all the help it needed and Mayor Nagin's outcry could have gone down as the definitive public display of black male rage in a time where anger was disappearing from black political expression. But just a day later, he'd be upstaged.

In the event of a natural disaster, network television stations do what they do best: host a telethon. A parade of stars lend their celebrity to the cause, appearing on television for a minute or two, either performing a sad song or reading an emotionally manipulative script, while encouraging viewers to donate to whatever large charity that has emerged as the point organization for that specific tragedy. On September 2, 2005, NBC simulcast *A Concert for Hurricane Relief* on NBC, MSNBC, and CNBC, while Faith Hill, Harry Connick Jr., Claire Danes, Hilary Swank, Lindsay Lohan, Leonardo DiCaprio, and others told of the dire situation in New Orleans that could only be helped if everyone donated to the American Red Cross Disaster Relief Fund.

And Kanye. *Late Registration* was set to be one of the biggest music releases of the year, selling over 800,000 copies during its first week in stores. It made sense to invite one of music's brightest stars, one who'd become known for a certain level of political consciousness at that, to a telethon in the wake of "the single most catastrophic natural disaster in U.S. history." But he was also Kanye West.

NBC paired him with Mike Myers, of *Saturday Night Live* and *Austin Powers* fame, who read the script from the teleprompter as any good celebrity telethon participant would. He told millions of people what happened to the levees, he told millions of people how dire the situation had become in New Orleans. And then it was Kanye's turn.

"I hate the way they portray us in the media. You see a black family, it says, 'They're looting.' You see a white family, it says, 'They're looking for food.' And, you know, it's been five days because most of the people are black. And even for me to complain about it, I would be a hypocrite because I've tried to turn away from the TV because it's too hard to watch. I've even been shopping before even giving a donation, so now I'm calling my business manager right now to see what is the biggest amount I can give, and just to imagine if I was down there, and those are my people down there. So anybody out there that wants to do anything that we can help—with the way America is set up to help the poor, the black people, the less well-off, as slow as possible. I mean, the Red Cross is doing everything they can. We already realize a lot of people that could help are at war right now, fighting another way— and they've given them permission to go down and shoot us."

While Kanye was speaking, you could see Mike Myers attempting to hide his discomfort while appearing sympathetic to Kanye's emotional, off-script rant about poor, dispossessed black people dying in the storm. And when it was his turn to speak again, Myers did what he could to get it back on track, to stick to the network television appeal for American charity. And then it was Kanye's turn.

"George Bush doesn't care about black people."

James Baldwin wrote in "Notes of a Native Son," "There is not a Negro alive who does not have this rage in his blood—one has the choice, merely, of living with it consciously or surrendering to it." In front of an audience of eight million, Kanye surrendered to it, and created perhaps the greatest moment in live television history. There was more script for Mike Myers to read, but he never got the chance, though given his double-take and fumbling afterward it's hard to tell if he would have gotten through the prepared remarks even if NBC hadn't cut away to Chris Tucker, who was equally flummoxed in another area of the studio. "George Bush doesn't care about black people." What made it perfect was that Kanye said it as if he was reading it from the teleprompter. Staring straight into the camera, his cadence straddled the line between stiff and natural—he looked and sounded like any person who wasn't accustomed to reading from a teleprompter would. But it was all Kanye. I couldn't have loved him any more. I was no longer alone.

Before then, the only times I had seen black men be angry in public were Allen Iverson's "we're talking about practice" press conference and any time my father received poor service at a restaurant. Politically speaking, Al Sharpton and Spike Lee seemed to be able to piss people off whenever they spoke, but their ubiquitous media presence had the effect of rendering their fiery personalities into punch lines. Rappers scowled a lot, but mostly at each other, and mostly over bullshit.

My nostalgia for a time period that I didn't live through had me wishing I grew up with a Malcolm X, Huey P. Newton, H. Rap Brown, Amiri Baraka, Stokely Carmichael (turned Kwame Ture), or Fred Hampton around to show me how black male rage could be harnessed as a weapon for revolution. Their teachings and inspiration reached me through reprinted texts and black-and-white documentary footage. I was being groomed to be a credit to my race, and a large part of that meant the rejection of the stereotypes imposed on our psyches, that of the Angry Black Man chief among them. Nearly every black elder in my life stressed how important it was to keep my composure, whatever the situation, because being labeled an Angry Black Man was a punishment akin to death. It would make white people uncomfortable, garner me a reputation as difficult to work with, stifle my professional opportunities, and ostracize me socially. I heard similar lectures after being a called a nigger in the sixth grade and cursing out three Marines. The objective was to always present oneself as being deserving of white people's respect. Anger belonged to thugs, menaces to society. I was to be a member of the talented tenth, and therefore my anger needed to be suppressed.

In less than two minutes, Kanye went from one of my favorite artists to one of my heroes because he didn't suppress it. He was young, black, and just didn't give a fuck on national television.

I carried that mentality with me into my second year of college. I joined the school newspaper, in earnest this time, and spent whatever time I wasn't attending political rallies to impress a girl on penning angry screeds about politics and culture for the opinion section of the Hampton Script.

I was fully committed to the idea of anger as a mobilizing force. I thought, after Kanye, everyone around me would understand and commit to it as well. I underestimated the appeal of hope.

It was pretty clear in the fall of 2006 that Barack Obama would be running for president. Politicians only write books when they're running for higher office or their political career is over. He was a first-term senator when *The Audacity of Hope* was released. Unless he was planning to torpedo everything and go back to community organizing in Chicago, there was only one direction his ambition pointed.

The month after *Audacity* came out, Sean Bell, Joseph Guzman, and Trent Benefield were shot at more than 50 times by five undercover police officers after coming out of a nightclub in Queens, New York. Bell was pronounced dead on arrival when his body reached the hospital, suffering gunshot wounds to the neck and arm. He was twenty-three years old, black, and unarmed. They all were.

On April 25, 2008, Michael Oliver, Gescard Isnora, and Marc Cooper—the three officers charged in the shooting—were acquitted on charges of manslaughter and reckless endangerment. The historic presidential race was in full swing at that point. On the campaign trail, Obama was asked for his reaction to the news of Sean Bell's killers being cleared of criminal responsibility:

"Well, look, obviously there was a tragedy in New York. I said at the time, without benefit of all the facts before me, that it looked like a possible case of excessive force. The judge has made his ruling, and we're a nation of laws, so we respect the verdict that came down. . . . The most important thing for people who are concerned about that shooting is to figure out how do we come together and assure those kinds of tragedies don't happen again. . . . Resorting to violence to express displeasure over a verdict is something that is completely unacceptable and counterproductive."

In fairness, there wasn't the same expectation for Democratic primary frontrunner Hillary Clinton to make a public statement on Sean Bell's killing and the subsequent acquittal of the police officers responsible for his death. Obama was the black candidate, even if he didn't want to be.

He'd made as much clear the month before in his Philadelphia speech. It's officially titled "A More Perfect Union," but it became informally known as the "Philadelphia race speech," the second-most important speech of Obama's national political career at that point. In July 2004 he introduced himself, and in March 2008 he solidified his identity.

The narrative of Obama at that point, despite having two books in circulation—one detailed memoir and one policy explainer—was that we didn't really know who he was. We, apparently, knew neither his biography nor his worldview, because two books and a series of primary debates provided no information. It was incumbent on the media to fill in the gaps.

So ABC News, venerable member of the fourth estate, reviewed tapes of Reverend Jeremiah Wright's sermons.

Wright served as pastor of Trinity United Church of Christ in Chicago. He married Barack and Michelle Obama and baptized their two daughters. Here lies the true key to understanding the potential president.

Wright said things like "We have supported state terrorism against the Palestinians and black South Africans, and now we are indignant because the stuff we have done overseas is now brought right back to our own front yards. America's chickens are coming home to roost" after 9/11, and "The government gives them the drugs, builds bigger prisons, passes a three-strike law and then wants us to sing 'God Bless America.' No, no, no, God damn America, that's in the Bible for killing innocent people. God damn America for treating our citizens as less than human. God damn America for as long as she acts like she is God and she is supreme" in 2003.

"I wouldn't call it radical," an anonymous Trinity member told ABC, "I call it being black in America."

But that couldn't be Obama's black. Obama's black needed to make white people comfortable enough to not see his blackness. He repudiated Wright's sermons, but even that wasn't enough to distance himself from his former pastor. Thus, the "Philadelphia race speech."

So many people called it brilliant that to hold an opposing view felt like being the one person saying "Elvis sucks" at Graceland. It was brilliant in the way political maneuvering is brilliant. As a statement on racism in America, however, that shit was straight garbage. But it showed that

Obama knew what was really at stake. His relationship to Rev. Wright wasn't under scrutiny because anyone actually believed the man might one day serve as chief of staff in the Obama White House. The threat Wright's theatrical and impassioned presence posed was the implication that Wright's presentation of the archetypal Angry Black Man might just be Obama's true identity. And an Angry Black Man could never be elected president.

In his speech, Obama explained that anger, while eagerly and eloquently distancing himself from it:

> For all those who scratched and clawed their way to get a piece of the American Dream, there were many who didn't make it—those who were ultimately defeated, in one way or another, by discrimination. That legacy of defeat was passed on to future generations—those young men and, increasingly, young women who we see standing on street corners or languishing in our prisons, without hope or prospects for the future. Even for those blacks who did make it, questions of race and racism continue to define their worldview in fundamental ways. For the men and women of Reverend Wright's generation, the memories of humiliation and doubt and fear have not gone away; nor has the anger and the bitterness of those years. That anger may not get expressed in public, in front of white co-workers or white friends. But it does find voice in the barbershop or the beauty shop or around the kitchen table. At times, that anger is exploited by

politicians, to gin up votes along racial lines, or to make up for a politician's own failings.

And occasionally it finds voice in the church on Sunday morning, in the pulpit and in the pews. The fact that so many people are surprised to hear that anger in some of Reverend Wright's sermons simply reminds us of the old truism that the most segregated hour of American life occurs on Sunday morning. That anger is not always productive; indeed, all too often it distracts attention from solving real problems; it keeps us from squarely facing our own complicity within the African-American community in our condition, and prevents the African-American community from forging the alliances it needs to bring about real change. But the anger is real; it is powerful. And to simply wish it away, to condemn it without understanding its roots, only serves to widen the chasm of misunderstanding that exists between the races.

He could have stopped there, and even with the unnecessary caveats about black anger distracting "attention from solving real problems," it would have been a perfectly acceptable liberal-minded statement on race in America. But Obama never missed an opportunity for a false equivalency. He continued:

In fact, a similar anger exists within segments of the white community. Most working- and middle-class white Americans don't feel that they have been particularly privileged by their race. Their experience is the immigrant experience—as far as they're concerned, no one handed them anything. They built it from scratch. They've worked hard all their lives, many times only to see their jobs shipped overseas or their pensions dumped after a lifetime of labor. They are anxious about their futures, and they feel their dreams slipping away. And in an era of stagnant wages and global competition, opportunity comes to be seen as a zero sum game, in which your dreams come at my expense. So when they are told to bus their children to a school across town; when they hear an African-American is getting an advantage in landing a good job or a spot in a good college because of an injustice that they themselves never committed; when they're told that their fears about crime in urban neighborhoods are somehow prejudiced, resentment builds over time.

It was as if he was reading the screenplay for Paul Haggis's *Crash*. This speech told White America that Obama believed that their racist anger is totally justified and not at all different from the anger of a population that has experienced racist discrimination and exploitation since they were brought to this country.

He also talked about his grandmother being racist. ABC News didn't do an exposé on Obama's affiliation with a known racist white person. Because learning about who/what influenced him was never the point.

The speech worked. Enough so, at least, that Obama was able to survive a similar attack tying him to Weather Underground cofounder Bill Ayers, and enough white people showed up to vote for him throughout the Democratic primary season and on election day. And Obama's ability to rise above it all, to persevere, gave way to an optimism among black Americans that threatened to make anger disappear from our politics altogether.

Which is understandable. Anger by itself is not sufficient. Anger is exhausting. After centuries of struggle, trading anger for hope is the sort of exhalation an oppressed people deserves. The hope of a black president for a people descended from those once held as property is the kind of story to make fairy tales jealous. But when things don't change, expecting those same people to continue hoping is to act as if those fairy tales are adequate substitutes for reality.

Obama's election crystallized the American narrative of progress—one that locates racial injustice in the past and as the product of ignorance and hatred—telling us that things will always get better. And yet the country, and black people specifically, experienced record levels of incarceration and unprecedented economic inequality. The symbolism of Obama's success became a cudgel against discussions of persistent racism in housing, education, and health care. And for the young people who showed up to the polls for the first time to put him into office, the limitations of having a black president gradually came to the fore.

One of Baldwin's most repeated quotes is: "To be a Negro in this country and to be relatively conscious is to be in a rage almost all the time." That rage can lay dormant at times, but then something unexpected will come along to jar it loose.

No one saw George Zimmerman killing Trayvon Martin coming. Nor the killing of Jordan Davis. Or Michael Brown, or Freddie Gray, or or or, so on and so on. Listing the names of our fallen starts to feel like a disservice to their memory, a hollow attempt at preservation. But their names kept coming to us, via state-sanctioned violence, one after the other, with little time to breathe in between. Wearing a hoodie. Carrying Skittles. Listening to loud music. Walking in the street. Running away. Minding their business. Unarmed. Killed. Each one nudging the anger of a new generation from dormant to active.

Black rage has long been a political tool. It has been used against us, but it is our anger, historically, that speaks to the core concerns of black people in America and provides a radical critique of the system of racism. Black rage announces itself at the Women's Convention in Akron, Ohio, and says, "Ain't I a woman?" Black rage stands before hundreds of thousands at the Lincoln Memorial and says, "America has given the Negro people a bad check, a check which has come back marked 'insufficient funds.'" Black rage says to the Democratic National Convention, "I'm sick and tired of being sick and tired." Black rage says "Fuck tha Police" and "Fight the Power." Or "George Bush doesn't care about black people."

But that anger has not only drawn attention to injustice; it has driven people to action, sparking movements and spurring them forward. At the very least, the public expression of black rage has allowed communities and people who have felt isolated in their own anger to know that they are not alone. Anger is what makes our struggle visible.

We almost lost that rage. We almost sacrificed it and its truth-telling abilities for a symbol of hope. And had we done so, choosing an option Baldwin hadn't imagined, America would have lost, too, its chance for redemption. Anger is what makes our struggle visible, and our struggle is what exposes the hypocrisy of a nation that fashions itself a moral leader. To rise against the narrative and expose the lie gives opportunity to those whose identity depends on the lie to question and, hopefully, change. Our struggle has inspired oppressed people the world over, because if we former slaves can make the most powerful nation face itself, there's a chance for everyone else. In a twist, our rage becomes hope for others. We almost gave it away.

Given the country's penchant for repression, though, our anger will never truly go away. Every now and then, we just need a little spark.

Chapter 3

Instead of returning to Walmart and watermelons in the summer of 2006, I went to Atlanta. I got an internship with the Dekalb County Board of Health, because a second cousin on my father's side used to work for them and exercised a certain amount of influence over the internship program. This meant getting out of Virginia and living on my own, for real this time. I'd lived on campus at Hampton for two years, but that summer was my first taste of young adult–style independence, complete with paying my own rent. I stayed in an apartment on Emory University's campus that it held specifically for students with internships in the Atlanta area.

It was the best and worst job ever. I worked in the environmental department and was tasked with West Nile virus prevention. What that meant was driving around the city to kill off mosquitoes by hitting all the freshwater locations with some kind of repellent. It was mind-numbing and, when I had to set traps near all the standing water, disgusting. But

I was making more money than I ever had. I drove around a few hours a day doing that and got paid almost eleven dollars an hour, which I thought was an insane amount, having come from my seven-and-change-an-hour job at Walmart. It more than paid for my rent and left me with the kind of disposable income you shouldn't trust in the hands of a nineteen-year-old.

It wasn't a job that fed my interests, though. There was nothing about it that helped me plan the revolution or hone my skills. I was thinking that maybe I wanted to be a writer, though I was still telling everyone I was going to be a lawyer. Being a lawyer sounded twice as good, like a job befitting a Black Leader, but coming off a year of anger-inflected opinion writing for the school paper, I was seeing a different path. With all the free time I had after work, I kept up my studies—reading the classic books, listening to the classic music, watching the classic films—and my writing. I filled up composition notebooks with awful poetry and attempts at rap lyrics, but also went online and posted semiconstructed essays on my MySpace blog.

But I was in Atlanta, the new Black Mecca, and I was not going to spend all of my time there in front of a computer. I'd never lived in a major city before. I was suddenly overwhelmed by all the entertainment options available. The highlights of my limited social life up to that point had been late-night IHOP trips and an off-campus house party at which one of the homies drunkenly broke his front teeth on the bathroom sink.

My main interest was all the concerts. Not that artists I was interested in seeing never came through Virginia Beach and the surrounding area, but Atlanta had several shows a week I wanted to see. I couldn't afford them all, having to feed myself and all that, but for a stretch I was going to a concert every other week. While online buying tickets for my first one (The Roots featuring Talib Kweli and Jean Grae, a dream lineup for my hip-hop-loving heart), I noticed that Dave Chappelle tickets were going on sale within the next few days. I hadn't even deposited my first paycheck yet but I knew there was no way I was going to miss Chappelle, who had become a model of black comedic brilliance—and for me, like a funnier version of Malcolm. Which is why I ended up praying to a God I wasn't sure existed when I got lost on the way to his show.

In the span of about three years, Chappelle had gone from The-Guy-from-*Half-Baked* to Funniest-Man-Alive to Enigmatic-Comedy-Legend. He made the first leap in 2003/4 with the premiere and success of *Chappelle's Show*. I remember learning The-Guy-from-*Half-Baked* was getting his own Comedy Central show because I was listening to *The Tom Joyner Morning Show*, Black America's favorite radio program (especially if you were born before 1970), while riding in the car with my mother. During this promotional interview, she heard Chappelle say he was from Washington, D.C., and decided she might have to give a brother from her hometown a shot. Then Tom Joyner asked him if it was true the show was going to feature "Nat King Cole booty videos" and my mother was instantly out. I, on the other hand, was all in.

I didn't know what to expect from the show as a whole, but I knew the point Chappelle was trying to make with the "Nat King Cole booty videos." It was his way of speaking back to the elders that constantly criticized hip-hop for its misogyny as if the problem started with rapping. In hindsight, he probably could/should have spent that time and energy actually addressing misogyny, but at the time I was filled with glee at Chappelle taking the pristine image of the most dignified, respectable symbol of black assimilation and muddying the established narratives of our cultural history, all in defense of hip-hop. He was a hero. But I wasn't yet sold on the show. That sketch was preceded by two passably amusing sketches that didn't make me laugh out loud and lacked the social commentary of the Nat King Cole sketch. It was followed by another kinda-sorta-maybe amusing sketch about having a stenographer record everyday conversations, but I wasn't sure if *Chappelle's Show* needed to be appointment viewing based on what I had seen. A few minutes later, when the line "I am in no way, shape, or form involved in any niggerdom!" was said on national television, however, everything changed.

In order to effectively execute a comedic sketch about a blind black man who is also a white supremacist, you have to possess a once-in-a-generation breed of genius that rattles the orthodoxy in all the necessary ways. Chappelle's Clayton Bigsby sketch showed he was that genius. Presented as a faux *Frontline* documentary, the sketch features interviews with Clayton Bigsby, the blind black man raised as a white who has, through his books and speeches, come to be a popular white supremacist thinker. He has choice hateful words to direct at "nigras, Jews, homosexuals, Mexicans, Arabs, and all kinds of different chinks" taking over America and "breathing all the white man's air." And they stink.

The sketch works because it wholly commits to absurdity, but the metaphor undergirding the absurdity is clear. The racist language is extreme, but the speaker has no ability to discern its truth because he literally can't see the world around him. How does he know black people "think they're the best dancers"? Someone had to tell him and he had to accept that as fact. It's how racist ideology is passed down. But when Bigsby finally learns that he is black and divorces his wife for being a "nigger lover," his hatred has been internalized to the point that he turns it on himself. It's a heady bit of comedy that could have been trapped by the need to shock, but it's Chappelle's genius that conveys the layers of the message in between gut-busting one-liners about "niggerdom."

Clayton Bigsby made Dave Chappelle, rather predictably, a controversial figure, and in the opening of the second episode of *Chappelle's Show*, he took some time to address the press's critical response:

That's the thing about being on TV, you just never can say what you wanna say, man. 'Cause if I said everything I thought it would just freak America out. You wouldn't wanna hear a young black dude saying half the things I be thinking. The only way people would listen to the stuff I think is if a pretty white girl sang my thoughts.

Chappelle would go on to produce a number of sketches over the next two years that are some of the greatest in comedy history. He influenced the way a generation spoke, introducing phrases to pop-culture lexicon that can still elicit laughter. But what happened next, when he brought a real-life pretty white girl on stage to sing his thoughts, defined the appeal of *Chappelle's Show*.

"Good evening, pretty white woman," he says. "Thank you for being here. I have some things I need to get off my chest." Chappelle starts to scribble on a notecard, while the white woman stands in her flowing gown, smiling unknowingly. He hands her the card and she starts to sing, operatically, what he's written down:

"Crack was invented and distributed to intentionally destroy the black community."

He hands her the next card:

"AIDS was too."

It continues:

"The police never looked for Tupac and Biggie's murderers.

"Fuck the police.

"What ever happened to that recount in Florida?

"O.J. didn't do it.

"On second thought, yeah he did.

"Gay sex is gross, sorry, I just find it to be gross.

"Unless of course they're leeeeeesssssbians.

"I like leeeeeesssssbians.

"I like leeeeeesssssbians."

Here, Chappelle cuts in to say, "For real nigga, I like lesbians. But I digress from my point." He returns to the notecards and the white woman returns to singing his thoughts:

"All Chinese people look alike.

"So do white people.

"Pretty much anyone who isn't black looks alike to me.

"Oh I want to stick my thumb in J. Lo's butt."

She hesitates a bit with the next card, but after some nudging from Chappelle, she goes on: "I wouldn't mind sticking a finger or two up that singing white girl's butt either.

"Call me on my cell, 917 . . ."

Chappelle stops her from reading the rest, indicating that it was only meant for her. She folds the notecard and places it in her cleavage. He returns to the cards, her to singing:

"And now it's time to collect ad revenue for Comedy Centralllllllll!!!!!!

"Revenue they don't share with my black ass."

This isn't the most popular *Chappelle's Show* moment, but it's the one that captures every bit of Chappelle's genius, as well as every shortcoming, that gave the show's short-lived existence the impact of eternity.

His statements about crack and AIDS, echoing the long-held beliefs of many in Black America that these devastating social ills were intentionally created with the destruction of black people in mind, established Chappelle as a race man with a perspective at odds with the mainstream. His mention of Tupac and Biggie and his cursing the police for never attempting to find their killers marked him as a member of the hip-hop generation, which offers a particular brand of defiance in the face of authority.

But when he gets to "gay sex is gross," Chappelle solidifies something assumed about "young black dudes" but normally unspoken. His heterosexual identity is assumed because unless gay is offered up as qualifier, we're given no reason to assume anything else. But when he said "gay sex is gross" Chappelle affirmed that identity and made "young black dude" mean something very specific. And he would never think of himself as being homophobic because he isn't revolted by the existence of gay people (which is why he follows his line with "sorry"), only the thought of them having sex, but it's something he can write off as a personal preference.

Unless, of course, they're lesbians. Because gay, for Chappelle, is only gross in the context of two men. Women engaged in same-sex relations are perfectly fine, because not only do they pose no threat to Chappelle's heterosexual identity, but relegating them to an erotic desire of his own only bolsters his hetero bona fides. If it wasn't clear before, it's clear now: Dave Chappelle is straight.

In the next bit, when he makes an admission of his own discriminatory beliefs—"all Chinese people look alike"—he establishes another identity: American. Chappelle shows how even he, as a black person and thus an outsider, is not immune to internalizing certain xenophobic tropes. When that's over, he's back to his heterosexual posturing, expressing his sexual fantasies about Jennifer Lopez and the white woman on stage singing his thoughts. The premise, again, is that no one wants to hear the thoughts of a young black dude, and even here this holds up, to a degree. A certain segment of America has no interest in hearing black men talk about their sexual desires, though they certainly project their own ideas about those desires onto us. But Chappelle's revelation was only rebellious if you'd never seen the "Big Pimpin'" video. In other words, he gave us more of the same black male heterosexual fantasizing we'd all grown wearily accustomed to.

When he reaches the end of this sketch and is sending the show off to a commercial break, he jokes about Comedy Central not sharing the ad revenue with him, alerting viewers to the exploitation of his labor. Chappelle was being paid, but he was no stranger to how capitalism collides with intellectual and artistic output. He created, wrote, produced, and starred in the show—he was the reason millions of people were watching Comedy Central at 10:30 on Wednesday nights—but ownership beats out labor every time. All the rights and licenses were stacked in Comedy Central's favor and they were under no obligation to share the revenue generated by Chappelle's show beyond his base salary.

This is true of all artists who make deals with large corporations, but when you're black in the entertainment business it comes with a reminder of the historical theft of your people's labor and creativity from Pat Boone to Vanilla Ice. Everyone has been able to profit from black genius except the actual black people responsible for that genius.

Chappelle wasn't supposed to say that, let alone say it on the network currently signing his checks. And, technically, he didn't. A singing white woman did. Maybe that's what eventually got Comedy Central to listen. The sketch is imperfect, but it accomplished its objective. The joke for the audience is that a young black dude could never get away with saying certain things on television. The joke on the industry is that he did.

But it's funny how one sketch can fuck up the game. Dave Chappelle spent that inaugural season of *Chappelle's Show* comedically dismantling racism, upending social conventions, making fun of popular culture, mishandling issues of gender, being blithely homophobic, and never shying away from poop jokes. The result was Comedy Central's most popular offering since the emergence of *South Park* and *The Daily Show*. The season one DVD release set sales records. Chappelle was the unofficial Funniest-Man-Alive, but with the second season the title would become undisputable. Everything the first season was, the second season was that but better. But among everything he created for us that year—a white family with the last name "Niggar," an indictment of racial disparities in our justice system, a rebuke of fast food companies that present their jobs as grand opportunities for young black men, a black version of George

Bush, and much more—the crown jewel, the thing that made him a mainstream superstar, was just four words: "I'm Rick James, bitch!"

The sketch was a different kind of absurd from blind-black-white-supremacist Clayton Bigsby. The premise was having frequent *Chappelle's Show* contributor Charlie Murphy, brother of comedy legend Eddie Murphy, tell true stories about hanging out with funk/soul/rock legend Rick James in the 1980s. James, as played by Chappelle, was fond of hard partying, hard drugging, hard fighting, and, apparently, frequently exclaiming, "I'm Rick James, bitch!"

That's it. They devoted an entire episode to telling variations of this story. It was undoubtedly hilarious, in that some of it seemed entirely too ridiculous to be true, but a passing familiarity with Rick James made it all plausible. No rational human being would go to Eddie Murphy's house and scream "fuck yo' couch, nigga, fuck yo' couch!" while digging their muddy boots into the seat cushions, but Rick James is no rational human being and cocaine is a helluva drug. And it wouldn't have worked if Chappelle, as he always did, hadn't committed to the absurdity.

The problem is that his genius was reduced to a catchphrase. I was a senior in high school when that sketch aired, and the next day at school all anyone could say to one another was "I'm Rick James, bitch!" We mumbled it underneath our breaths in response to questions from teachers, we said it apropos of nothing in the lunchroom, we yelled it in the hallways when we thought we wouldn't get caught. It didn't mean anything, but it was our universal cultural connection for that moment.

But when an artist, especially one of Chappelle's genius, is stripped down to a meaningless catchphrase, it's an insult to their body of work. He was working hard to have his art respected in an industry that disposes of the talents of young black dudes without so much as brushing the dirt from its shoulders. Here he was being told that his worth wasn't his intelligence or creativity, but his ability to mimic a famous person shouting obscenities. It was the popularity of the Rick James sketch that set him on the path toward South Africa.

"The show is ruining my life," he told an audience in Sacramento that wouldn't stop screaming "I'm Rick James, bitch!" while he attempted to do his stand-up act. He added:

> You know why my show is good? Because the network officials say you're not smart enough to get what I'm doing, and every day I fight for you. I tell them how smart you are. Turns out, I was wrong. You people are stupid.

On top of that, he wasn't being paid what he was worth. He reportedly made about $90,000 an episode for the second season and saw a small percentage of his record-breaking DVD sales. Comedy Central was making millions on millions in revenue—revenue they weren't sharing with Dave's black ass. For him to continue producing a show that was ruining his life and was being watched by stupid people, it would take a raise that reflected his status as Funniest-Man-Alive.

Maybe he sent the singing white woman in to do nego-
tiations for him, because Comedy Central heard him, to the
tune of about $55 million for the production of two seasons,
as well as a bigger share of DVD sales. Chappelle was going
to return in the spring of 2005, after a disappointing presidential election and the dawn of the Age of Obama, to give
us more of the thoughts from a young black dude that were
never supposed to make it on television. He'd just be a lot
richer this go-around.

Except it never happened. Instead of continuing to be the
Funniest-Man-Alive, Chappelle chose to become an Enigmatic-Comedy-Legend. In a decision he'd spend the next
decade trying to explain, he walked away from the production of season three, away from $55 million, and flew to
South Africa.

Was he on drugs? Was he crazy? These seemed the only
reasons any of us, as fans, could come up with as to why any
rational person would fly eight thousand miles away from
$55 million. And in such dramatic fashion. He went to
South Africa by himself, telling no one, and didn't return
for two weeks. Speculation was all we had, even when he
did come back to the United States, and our speculation
was rooted in our own greed. Chappelle had achieved the
dream—fame and fortune and respect—as far as we could
see, so anything short of an insanity defense would be
deemed inadmissible.

But when he started opening up about his decision at the
beginning of the next year, Dave showed he possessed a

deeper commitment to the social consciousness many of us as fans only professed by way of watching his show. He granted his very first interview to Oprah. It aired on February 3, 2006. I skipped classes that day to ensure I'd be in my dorm room and able to watch. She wasted no time in getting to the question that was on everyone's mind: "Why did you walk away from $50 million?"

The look on his face was more pensive than I was accustomed to. Dave Chappelle has a face created for comedy. That might sound like a dis, but there's something naturally mischievous about his face. His every grin and reaction and contortion looks as if he's gleefully getting away with something. All of that had been stripped away.

"I wasn't walking away from the money," he said, "I was walking away from the circumstances that were coming with the newfound plateau. . . . When you're a guy that generates money, people have a vested interest in trying to control you."

For a while he spoke as if he didn't fully understand yet why he had walked away. He was still trying to put words to a feeling that the rest of us couldn't understand either. The longer he talked, though, the more he became settled in his truth.

"I was doing sketches that were funny, but were socially irresponsible," Dave said. "I felt like I was deliberately being encouraged and I was overwhelmed. It's like you're getting flooded with things and you don't pay attention to things like your ethics when you get so overwhelmed."

But it wasn't the material that was changing. *Chappelle's Show* courted controversy by design. You could always tell, from those mischievous contortions, that Dave reveled in his ability to offend week after week. You don't make parody music videos of R. Kelly singing about peeing on people and not know exactly what you're doing. It's different, though, when you think the audience is keeping up with you, that they understand the subversion. "What I didn't consider was how many people watch the show and how the way people use television is subjective," he told Oprah. He was trapped by his own popularity. He wasn't giving these sketches to the people who got it anymore. He was performing for people who wanted to shout "I'm Rick James, bitch!" at him on the street. People operating on that level could easily misconstrue his artistic intentions.

He recalled filming a sketch that featured a character in blackface (a "visual representation of the n-word," as Dave put it) and seeing a white guy working on set laugh a little too hard. "It was the first time I ever got a laugh that I was uncomfortable with," he said. What's worse is that he felt it was the kind of laughter the people around him—studio executives, writers, et cetera—were encouraging, and now that he was generating more money than before, he couldn't afford to worry about morality and ethics. He needed to make the show more popular, generate more cash, and ensure that everyone whose name wasn't on the marquee continued to profit from him.

"I love being famous, it's phenomenal," Dave explained to Oprah, "it's the way the people around you position themselves around you to get into your pockets and into your mind. That is infuriating."

"The truth is that we get a little disappointed when our geniuses are fully in control of their gifts," historian and cultural critic Jelani Cobb wrote in his essay "The Devil and Dave Chappelle." That's doubly true for black men who aren't supposed to possess those gifts in the first place. We're expected to give freely of ourselves and be grateful that anyone is even paying attention.

"The hardest thing to do is to be true to yourself, especially when everybody is watching," Dave told Oprah. So the question becomes: How much of yourself are you willing to sell in order to be seen?

I didn't come away with a clear answer for myself after watching the interview. Seeing Dave Chappelle's saga unfold while harboring a desire for a writing career where my still-evolving politics would be at the center, I knew I could one day face that kind of conflict, in this world where young black dudes aren't supposed to say certain things in public. You can choose to say them anyway, and have an audience as big as my MySpace blog, with just as much income as it generated. Or you can go along to get along, taking what's available and paying and comfortable, and drive around killing off mosquitoes. Or you can mute parts of yourself in pursuit of your passion, hoping that opens up greater opportunities and platforms, which is what I felt myself doing as I prepared to transition from opinion writer to opinion editor.

Dave Chappelle was the only person I knew of who was actively wrestling with a similar conundrum. I felt I needed him to help guide me through the uncertain answers.

On June 18, 2006, however, as I was driving to his show, I just needed someone to guide me off the highway, and I was hoping the God I wasn't sure existed would provide some assistance. I have a notoriously bad sense of direction and the Atlanta traffic didn't make it easy for me. I was relying on MapQuest to get me everywhere I needed to be that summer and still getting lost. I thought, though, that I could handle getting myself to the Dave Chappelle show. I had driven to the venue before, when I went to see The Roots and Talib Kweli, and the directions were fairly simple. An hour later, I was crying and praying behind the steering wheel of my Toyota Corolla, thinking I'd missed my chance to sit with Dave's wisdom.

Panicking when there is no cause for it is one of my trademark characteristics. I pulled over for a while, composed myself, wiped my tears on my new outfit, and realized that I was only about a five-minute drive from where I needed to be. I found a parking space and rushed over, thirty minutes late, believing I had missed half of Dave's set, but glad to catch any glimpse of him I could.

I showed my ticket and walked down to my second-row seat with my hands rattling. Dave hadn't hit the stage yet, and wouldn't for another half hour. From the door I heard a familiar voice, one I'd pressed play on too many times to count. I couldn't calm my hands down or accept what my eyes were telling was true until I sat down. Mos Def was there. With a microphone in his hand. Performing. Opening up for Dave Chappelle. I may have thought of those two as gods before, but for a moment the idea of God gained a little more credibility.

Mos Def did renditions of his biggest hits, "Ms. Fat Booty" and "Umi Says," that threatened to ruin the recorded versions for me, interspersed with his own amateur stand-up routine. I couldn't stop smiling. I'm not one to express joy very often, but I sat there with the stupidest, cheesiest grin on my face. Then Dave walked across stage, embraced Mos Def, and basked in the glow of his standing ovation. It was a perfect moment.

The mischief was back. For the first fifty minutes of the set, you might have forgotten that this was a man so stressed out by the accompaniments to fame and fortune that he needed to escape to South Africa just to clear his head. He was back in his element, moving effortlessly through jokes about American slavery, meth addiction, Father's Day, and masturbation. But he knew why we were there. "I was scared nobody would show up," he said after a while. "I thought y'all be mad, like, 'Nigga, how the fuck you gon' walk away from $50 million???'" We had heard him tell the story on Oprah, but for people invested in him as more than a comedian and entertainer, it lacked intimacy. We were there for Dave as a truth-telling prophet of our times. And Dave knew. The house lights dimmed, he sat on a stool, and he told us the truth.

Before him, Paul Robeson told the truth. As did Harry Belafonte, Dick Gregory, and Ossie Davis. And Richard Pryor. Chappelle was much more like Pryor than the others, as neither would be considered much of an activist, but the thing they all have in common is that they used the attention and respect afforded them through their artistry and celebrity to draw attention to injustice. They didn't take lightly the idea of social responsibility.

But as tempting as it is to get nostalgic for a time when black artists and celebrities were more militant, more involved, more outspoken, more political, there is no history where such a broad stroke applies. For every Paul Robeson, there's a Nat King Cole. For every Dick Gregory, there's a Bill Cosby. For every Richard Pryor, there's a Flip Wilson. And as the entertainment industry grew and more money was at stake, and our organized political movements were dismantled or withered away, there were even fewer Harry Belafontes. The 1980s gave rise to a whole host of apolitical black megastars who had benefited from the movements their idols were involved in during the 1960s and '70s, but who felt no obligation or desire to stand in that tradition. No one was more emblematic of this particular ethos than Michael Jordan.

Like millions of other kids of the late 1980s/early 1990s, I fell for the greatest marketing scheme of all time and wanted to "Be Like Mike." I couldn't always convince my parents to spend eighty dollars on the newest Air Jordan sneakers, but I could take to my driveway basketball hoop and try to hit the fadeaway jumper with my tongue hanging out. Jordan's lack of political mettle was irrelevant to me at the time. The multicultural '90s were teaching us impressionable children that racism was over. We learned all about color-blindness and Dr. King's dream of being judged by our character, not our skin tone. There was nothing left, in terms of racism, for us to fight against. Whatever obstacles existed were of our own making, and if we were willing to put in the work, like Mike, we could succeed at anything.

"Jordan was in many ways the fruit of the Civil Rights movement, which reached its apex in the year of his birth," *New York Times* sports columnist William Rhoden wrote in his controversial bestseller *Forty Million Dollar Slaves*. "His right to remain silent is what we won. Jordan didn't have an obligation to speak up on racial injustices, but he had an unmatched opportunity."

Jordan became the world's most popular athlete in the decade after Muhammad Ali held that title. They couldn't be more different, except in the fact that they were both black men. That isn't insignificant. They were the most visible black men in the world and used that platform in vastly different ways. Ali spoke to the condition of his people in the United States, becoming an ambassador for human rights the world over while remaining rooted in a black American tradition of resistance. Jordan sold sneakers. As American sports culture became more wedded to corporate culture and mass marketing, Jordan's fame and influence surpassed that of Ali's. In the process he spawned a generation of imitators, everyone from groundbreaking golfer Tiger Woods to Michael Jordan clone Kobe Bryant, both of whom steered away from any explicit political stances.

While there was never a critical mass of athlete-activists, it was at least more likely before the Jordan era. But His Airness showed just how much money and fame there was to be gained in neutrality. Athletes who did choose to speak out—notably Jordan's Chicago Bulls teammate Craig Hodges hand delivering a letter to President George H. W. Bush about the treatment of poor and minority communities, and Denver Nuggets point guard Mahmoud Abdul-Rauf refusing to stand for the national anthem and calling the flag a symbol of oppression—became cautionary tales because it effectively ended their careers. "It is unusual for athletes to take an active role in anything that might threaten . . . a contract," Rhoden wrote. In the Jordan era, the idea of seeing a photo like the one of Jim Brown, Bill Russell, and Kareem Abdul-Jabbar (then named Lew Alcindor) flanking Muhammad Ali during a press conference to support Ali's refusal to be drafted into the U.S. Army was basically unthinkable.

It was more than a symbolic changing of the guard when Jordan retired from basketball, for the third and final time, in 2003 and LeBron James was drafted number one by the Cleveland Cavaliers. LeBron was Cleveland's revenge. Part of the Jordan legacy is the ways in which he routinely torched Cleveland, famously dashing their playoff aspirations in 1989 with a last-second shot now immortalized in highlight reels and retrospectives. It was only a part of the city of Cleveland's sports woes, having not won a championship in any major sport since Jim Brown was a running back with the Cleveland Browns in 1964. LeBron wasn't just the latest greatest hope for winning, he was also the heir apparent to the throne vacated by Jordan—the best and most popular basketball player in the world—and what sweet revenge it would be to host him in Cleveland.

All he had to do was fit into the mold. Initially, there was nothing to suggest that James would do anything but fall right into the post-Jordan pack. Straight out of high school, he signed a $90 million endorsement deal with Nike, before he even had an NBA contract offer. His career hadn't started and there were already millions at risk. And then he added other big names with McDonald's and Coca-Cola. Poised to become the next big thing in the world of sports, there was every incentive for LeBron James to mimic Michael Jordan on and off the court. He even wore "23" on his jersey.

The first sign that he was different came when he campaigned for Barack Obama's 2008 presidential run. It was by no means a radical stance, but compared to Jordan's assertion that "Republicans buy sneakers, too," when he was asked to endorse (black, Democrat, former mayor of Charlotte, North Carolina) Harvey Gantt's Senate run in 1990, it was damn near revolutionary. LeBron had sneakers to sell, too, but it didn't prevent him from throwing his celebrity into the political world. After Obama won, James told the Associated Press, "It was uplifting. It was something that you can tell your kids, you really can become anything now. You don't have to become a basketball player. You can become president of the United States." He didn't say it explicitly, but the "black kids" was implied.

For such a highly paid, highly visible, perennial All-Star with numerous high-profile endorsements to even hint at a having a political ideology and race consciousness was meaningful. LeBron, for all of the comparisons he was drawing to Jordan on the court, was separating himself from Jordan's meticulously constructed persona off of it.

Which is why The Decision shouldn't have come as such a shock. Not only the actual decision he made to leave Cleveland and play for the Miami Heat, but the spectacle of it all. LeBron started getting national media attention at age fifteen and had been called by his nickname "King James" since he was sixteen years old. Of course he thought we wanted to watch an hour-long production of him making a career decision. We had been telling him we did for years.

About thirteen million people tuned in to ESPN on July 8, 2010, to watch The Decision special. LeBron was putting an end to chatter about where he would play after declaring his free agency at the end of the 2009–10 season. He didn't need to make the announcement via live television, during primetime, with ESPN giving away the airtime and all the ad revenue being donated to various charities, including the Boys and Girls Club. But he did.

"In this fall . . . this is very tough . . . in this fall I'm going to take my talents to South Beach and join the Miami Heat," he said about thirty minutes into the special. He wanted to win championships and he felt that playing in Miami, alongside his friends Dwyane Wade and Chris Bosh, would give him the best chance to do so. Citizens of the city of Cleveland responded by burning LeBron James jerseys in the street.

Shortly after The Decision was announced, Cavaliers majority owner Dan Gilbert posted a letter to the fans on the team's website. It read, in part:

> As you now know, our former hero, who grew up in the very region that he deserted this evening, is no longer a Cleveland Cavalier.
>
> This was announced with a several day, narcissistic, self-promotional build-up culminating with a national TV special of his "decision" unlike anything ever "witnessed" in the history of sports and probably the history of entertainment.
>
> Clearly, this is bitterly disappointing to all of us. . . .
>
> You simply don't deserve this kind of cowardly betrayal. . . .
>
> I can tell you that this shameful display of selfishness and betrayal by one of our very own has shifted our "motivation" to previously unknown and previously never experienced levels. . . .

This shocking act of disloyalty from our home grown "chosen one" sends the exact opposite lesson of what we would want our children to learn.

Narcissistic. Cowardly. Shameful. Selfish. Disloyal. All the man did was decide where and under what conditions he wanted to work. But here, he wasn't a man. Entertainers cease being people to us once they're on the screen. Moreover, they no longer belong to themselves—they're ours. In sports, where the personality and wallets of team owners are as much a part of the game as the players on the field, that dynamic is more pronounced. Our social contract defines athletes as well-compensated pieces of property, not workers with rights. For black athletes, this calls back to an ugly history.

This is what Rhoden was getting at with *Forty Million Dollar Slaves*, though his title likely prevented many from understanding his point. No, millionaire athletes are not literally enslaved. And for some, the analogy of slavery should never be deployed as a rhetorical device, given that the brutality of what our ancestors endured is hardly comparable to anything we experience today.

It's a point well taken, even if I don't wholeheartedly agree. An analogy isn't meant to be exact, but it should reflect some truth. It may be hyperbolic to suggest, as Jesse Jackson did, that Gilbert saw "LeBron as a runaway slave," but why did he consider it a "cowardly betrayal" for a man to choose where he wanted to work? What's "shameful" about choosing to be paid for your talents under working conditions that you have a final say over? And can anyone imagine Gilbert saying these things about a white guy?

Or the sports media and fans vilifying someone like Tom Brady for doing what LeBron did? "I think so, at times," LeBron said when asked by CNN's Soledad O'Brien if race played a role in the way The Decision was received. "There's always—you know, a race factor." Black athletes aren't meant to advocate for themselves. They aren't supposed to see their success as a result of their skills, dedication, hard work, persistence, and sacrifice. Their money and fame are gifts bestowed upon them by benevolent owners and fans, for which they should be grateful and constantly show gratitude. And loyalty. Loyalty above all else. Because without the salvation of sports, LeBron, born a black boy in America, would only have had two choices: cog or killer.

But LeBron rejected this. He didn't do anything radical, like build an all-new basketball league where players are owners and receive all of the profit derived from their talents and likenesses. But he, along with Wade and Bosh, built on Curt Flood's assertion that athletes have the right to work where they choose. As a result, he was called a narcissist. Certainly he could have done all of this without an hour-long ESPN special. But why? The Decision was ostentatious if you believe a man who spent his entire adult life being called "King" was supposed to exist in humility. Black men can celebrate themselves. LeBron saw Kanye, too.

This is why the Michael Jordan model has been comforting to America, especially after the disruptive 1960s and '70s era of black athletes. The endorsements were meant to buy silence. Jordan took the money, played the game, and sold the sneakers. LeBron James has taken the money, played the game, sold the sneakers, and refused to shrink. Visible black men no longer have to be silent. LeBron saw Kanye, too.

LeBron created a new model. He's not Rube Foster starting the Negro National League or Muhammad Ali critiquing American imperialism, nor is he Michael "Republicans buy sneakers, too," Jordan. He's somewhere at the nexus of all these philosophies, covered in tattoos, Allen Iverson style. He has exhibited a great awareness of his position as a highly visible black man and not shirked the idea that it comes with some social responsibility. Much like Dave Chappelle, only with less South Africa.

Their two differing trajectories illuminate two important lessons about how to navigate the economy of commodification: knowing your price and knowing your worth. The truth Dave shared with us while sitting underneath that spotlight in Atlanta was that someone, some industry, is always ready and waiting to exploit us. It appears innocent enough at first. They even convince us that the arrangement is beneficial for everyone involved. But once you realize what's happening, that they aren't sacrificing nearly as much as you are but somehow receiving a larger portion of the spoils, and you confront them about it, they'll try to convince you that you're crazy. Where they once sold you on the relationship with promises of wealth, they now threaten you with poverty. And they're willing to employ depraved measures in order show you just how bloody life is without them. When you recognize this, you have to make a choice: fight or run.

Dave showed you could fight by running. Not as a coward, but as a principled person. The price was too high and not high enough. He would have had to sell too much of himself that even $50 million couldn't buy.

LeBron has approached it differently. He started with different goals. Early in his career he said he wanted to be the richest man in the world. No one gets that rich by fighting or running. But when you also understand your fame as a responsibility, as LeBron does, you have to make different kinds of choices. He knows what he's worth—I'm sure in some spiritual sense, but here I mean straight dollars. He generates millions for lots of people. And so long as he's the best and most popular basketball player in the NBA, he'll continue to be worth millions for those people. The price he makes them pay is giving millions to a man who won't be silenced.

This was most clear a month after George Zimmerman killed Trayvon Martin. Black America was mourning. Black Twitter was marching. Black celebrities were hiding. LeBron James and his Miami Heat teammates specifically were being called out via Black Twitter. Not only was Trayvon from Miami, where LeBron had chosen to take his talents, Zimmerman had killed him while he was on his way back home to watch the best, most popular basketball player in the world finish playing the All-Star game. It was too close to home for LeBron to ignore.

And he listened. LeBron organized his twelve teammates and they took a photo. He posted the picture to Twitter with the accompanying hashtags *#WeAreTrayvonMartin*, *#Hoodies*, *#Stereotyped*, and *#WeWantJustice*. They stood there—rich, famous, black—with their hoodies covering their heads and asked the world to see them as Trayvon Martin. They asked for justice.

All the tears I'd held back for weeks came flowing the moment I saw it. For years, I envied the generation that had the image of John Carlos and Tommie Smith raising their Black Power fists at the 1968 Olympics to call their own. Now, I had mine. I had athletes who, with much to lose, would put their visibility to use for the liberation of black people. They saw enough of themselves in Trayvon to get off the fence and into the fight. There was hope again.

But also deep sadness. For all the hope the picture represented, there was always this reality to return to: there will be more Trayvon Martins than LeBron Jameses. LeBron's ability to choose millions and his voice, and Chappelle's choice of sanity and independence, are inspiring. But choice is a privilege not afforded most black boys trying to become black men in America. We can't all dribble a basketball, make people laugh, rap on beat—or write. We don't all have talents someone, some industry wants to exploit. Most of us have our bodies, our minds if we're lucky, and a desire to survive against the odds. Choices are a privilege defined by circumstance. In this country, the circumstance is always racism, oftentimes poverty. The two combined strip our choices away to the minimum.

The hope represented in Chappelle's trip to South Africa and LeBron making The Decision, though, is that those choices will be given back to all of us.

God willing.

Chapter 4

H ampton University was founded as Hampton Normal and
Agricultural Institute in 1868 by General Samuel Chap-
man Armstrong, a man described to me as a racist. That's
not something they were putting in the promotional bro-
chure, but my University 101 (a mandatory class designed as
part Hampton University history lesson, part semester-long
orientation) professor felt it was important for incoming
freshmen to know. It's not settled history that Armstrong
was a racist, but this professor's argument was that the former Union Army general's paternalism qualified. The way
he explained it, Armstrong's interest in establishing Hampton Institute rested on his belief that the newly freed black
population would be incapable of self-sufficiency without
strong (white) guidance. Armstrong's own statement of purpose reads: "The thing to be done was clear: to train selected
Negro youth who should go out and teach and lead their
people first by example, by getting land and homes; to give

them not a dollar that they could earn for themselves; to teach respect for labor, to replace stupid drudgery with skilled hands, and in this way to build up an industrial system for the sake not only of self-support and intelligent labor, but also for the sake of character."

Whether that makes him a racist is certainly debatable, but any person who believes they have to instill "respect for labor" in formerly enslaved people does not regard those people very highly.

I didn't know this origin story when I decided to apply to Hampton. What I knew was that the school fit my criteria: it was a historically black college (HBCU) that I could get into even without a bunch of extracurricular activities on my resume. I visited the campus once before deciding Hampton would be it, based on my highly sophisticated decision-making rationale: it just felt right, ya know?

It did until it didn't. After spending my first year silently assuming I was smarter and better than everyone else, making few attempts at friendship, and losing my scholarship, I returned the next year determined to socialize more. I joined the newspaper and political science club, which meant there were going to be at least two nights a week where I'd leave my dorm room, go to meetings, and be around other people with similar interests. And while I didn't exactly find a tribe of kindred spirits, I got to know people based on whether they were kind listeners, had warm laughs and quick wit, and stopped judging them based on whether they also had an unread copy of *Wretched of the Earth* lying around.

Writing opinion pieces for the student-run newspaper, the *Hampton Script*, helped me open up more. It always felt odd when people stopped me on campus to say they liked an article I had written. I wondered how they knew who I was, since my face wasn't next to my byline and I was convinced I was moving around in stealth, but it provided a little ego boost to know I'd written something other people were enjoying.

The first thing I wrote that year was an anti-BET screed, a la Aaron McGruder. The network had just recently banned a music video from legendary hip-hop group De La Soul, for reasons that were unclear, but continued playing the same fourteen ass-shaking videos from four different rappers on a loop. De La represented everything we '80s babies were told was "real" about hip-hop culture, so with their godlike status it was a sacrilege for BET to ban their video, a real slap in the face to anyone who was committed to keeping the culture alive and authentic. I was surprised the editors let me write the piece, but from then on I knew I'd be able to express myself without too much interference. I covered all my interests that year—national politics, hip-hop, sports, hating Valentine's Day—and became enough of a presence on the opinion page and in the newspaper office to convince everyone that I was the logical choice for opinion editor for the next year.

That's when I threw myself completely into the *Hampton Script*. I was also vice president of the political science club, but with the increasing hours at the newspaper and my waning romantic interest in Sharita, I eventually abandoned that post and made the *Script* my life. I wasn't required to, but I wanted to stay in the office until the entire paper was done and sent off to the printer. I asked the associate editor to teach me about laying out a page and converting it to PDF, how to place ads, what wire service we used, where the paper was printed, when it was delivered, and where we should place it for everyone to see. The *Script* meant a lot to me. It was where my words were.

Those long hours spent with the staff gave me some of my first true friendships, my first love, and crucial lessons about openness and vulnerability. I was like a little kid who thinks they can feel themselves growing taller. But it was real. I felt myself growing as a person.

My grades were the best they had ever been that year. My father thought it was the influence of Leslie, my straight-A physics major girlfriend. Luckily she had never judged me based on my ambivalence toward homework and turning assignments in on time. It wasn't about her, though. I had found my place. I was finding my voice. The *Hampton Script*, my column, my colleagues, my readers, and the writers working under me all inspired a shift in confidence that spilled out into all areas of my life.

It was only natural, then, that I would go for the top job, editor in chief, for my senior year. The whole staff presumed I would. I took it seriously enough to actually put on a suit for the interview. I went before the advisory board (the *Hampton Script* was not an independent publication), which consisted of the dean of students and a selection of random administrators whose journalism experience ranged from little to none at all. I thought maybe I had messed up the interview when I got some pushback for saying Don Imus should have been fired for his "nappy-headed hoes" comment (probably the first red flag I should have paid some attention to), but ultimately they gave me the job, despite their misgivings that I wasn't a journalism major. It wasn't really that difficult of a decision. I was the only one interested.

Regardless, I was excited. I called my mother as soon as I found out and she exceeded my excitement, as she always had, in her congratulations. I called my father soon after. "You're going to be editor in chief of the paper? Ah. Okay." My smile dimmed a bit, but it wasn't as if I didn't see it coming. I was still telling him I was going to law school. He had beamed at that news. Had I called him with news that I'd gotten straight As and was applying early for Harvard Law, he would have thrown his whole being into supporting me. That was something he understood.

But I wasn't going to let his lack of enthusiasm diminish mine. This was the moment I had waited for. I was never going to be the speechifying type, with my anxiety around public speaking, but I knew I'd be capable of penning the words to move millions. Or, for the time being, a couple thousand.

I returned to my cushy summer internship in Atlanta (instead of killing mosquitoes, this time around I was inspecting pools), where my lax work schedule allowed me to devote more time to preparing for my new role with the *Script*. Outside of making sure my little brother didn't die, I had never carried this much responsibility. My new confidence levels were being tested by the demands of leadership. I had my passions, but the paper didn't consist of twelve broadsheet pages of opinions on black culture and racism in America. There was the Campus section, with all the vital news the student body needed to know about campus life. I hadn't been that social or involved, so I had no idea how to handle that. There was the Lifestyle section, which mostly reported about the latest trends in beauty and fashion. At the time, my daily uniform was a polo shirt and Puma sneakers. But everyone was going to be looking to me for guidance, for some kind of vision as to how to create a newspaper that Hampton students would actually read and hopefully win some awards. It was my job to create that vision and get everyone on board. By June, I was panicking.

Then in July, Leslie asked me if I had heard about the Jena Six. I hadn't. We were talking over AOL Instant Messenger, so she immediately sent me a link to an article she had read. When I finished reading it, I immediately called her, even though I didn't have anything to say. I had grunts and screams and fucks, but no valuable thoughts. But Leslie saw what I saw, so I didn't need any words. She understood.

The piece was called "Injustice in Jena as Nooses Hang from the 'White Tree,'" written by human-rights lawyer and

Loyola University law professor Bill Quigley for Truth-out. org. It was a story about how Robert Bailey, Carwin Jones, Bryant Purvis, Jesse Ray Beard, Theo Shaw, and Mychal Bell came to be charged with attempted murder in the town of Jena, Louisiana.

On December 4, 2006, the six boys, with ages ranging from fourteen to eighteen, beat up a white classmate, in what was being reported as the culmination of several months of racial tension that had been rising at Jena High School. The beginning, according to Quigley, was in September of that year, when a black student asked the principal if he was allowed to sit under the tree in the school's courtyard that was known as the "white tree." The principal told him he could sit wherever he wanted. So he did.

The next day, students found nooses hanging from the tree. According to Quigley, the white students responsible received a light suspension. At a school assembly following the incident, a white district attorney gave a speech addressing the entire student body, but reportedly singled out the black students who were upset about the nooses, and told them, "I can be your best friend or your worst enemy. I can take away your lives with a stroke of my pen."

Then in December, Quigely wrote, "a black student who showed up at a white party was beaten by whites. On Saturday, December 2, a young white man pulled out a shotgun in a confrontation with young black men at the Gotta Go convenience store outside Jena before the men wrestled it away from him. The black men who took the shotgun away were later arrested; no charges were filed against the white man." On December 4, Bailey, Jones, Purvis, Beard, Shaw, and Bell were involved in the altercation that led to them becoming known as the Jena Six. Justin Barker, a seventeen-year-old white student at Jena High School, was on the receiving end of punches, kicks, and stomps that sent him to the hospital. But his injuries, according to Quigley's description, weren't that serious, as Barker "was taken to the hospital, treated, and released. He attended a social function that evening." Barker was also supposed to have made racist jokes that included slurs, prompting the beating.

Many of the details of this time line have been contested. According to reporting from Craig Franklin, assistant editor of the *Jena Times*, there was no "white tree." White and black students alike had always sat under the tree in question. An investigation into the hanging of the nooses found that it was a prank carried out by the rodeo team, who apparently had no understanding of the history of lynching and the symbolism of nooses. The white district attorney, Reed Walters, was said to have directed his "I can be your best friend or your worst enemy" comment not at the black students but at some white girls who were preoccupied with their cell phones during his school assembly address. Robert Bailey had been involved in a fight at a party on December 1, but Franklin reports it was erroneously referred to as an all-white party. Bailey was involved in the incident the next day at the Gotta Go convenience store, though there are conflicting testimonies as to what transpired between him and his companions and the white men who were not Jena students. And as far as the fight itself, the boys later admitted that Barker had not told any racist jokes or used any slurs, though it remained unclear if the motivation for the beating had anything to do with the nooses from September. Barker's injuries, meanwhile, had perhaps been severely downplayed; the Associated Press reported that a photo shown in court that had been taken while Barker was in the hospital revealed a "badly swollen face with one blackened eye swollen completely shut."

Parsing the details of any event that relies heavily on eyewitness accounts is difficult, but what was not in dispute was this: by the time I read Quigley's original article, Mychal Bell, then seventeen years old, had been tried and convicted, as an adult, for the lesser but still serious felony charges of aggravated battery and conspiracy to commit aggravated battery. He faced up to twenty-two years in prison and would be sentenced on September 20, 2007.

My father told me my namesake was Mychal Thompson, the Bahamian-born NBA player who had been the number one overall pick in the 1978 draft, making history as the first foreign-born player to be selected first. He had a solid career, not Hall of Fame caliber, but managed to win a couple of championships with the Los Angeles Lakers in '87 and '88. I never asked why my parents chose to spell my name the way they did, I just liked the feeling of uniqueness it gave me. There were always going to be Michaels, but I had never met another Mychal, and that marked me as special.

Mychal Bell was the first fellow Mychal I'd come across. The injustice of him facing twenty-two years in prison for what I then thought was a schoolyard fight filled me with a familiar rage, but his name left me with nothing more than the unintelligible grunts and screams and fucks that only Leslie understood. I was looking at Mychal Bell and seeing myself. Intellectually, I had always understood that by virtue of being a young black man in America there was no safety, that by bullet or gavel my life could be taken away. That fear was always following me, but as a black middle-class college kid at Hampton, the combination of class and educational privilege provided me with a false sense of exemption. I *could* get shot, I *could* get arrested, but I wouldn't because I was one of the chosen. I was exceptional. I was one of the tokens that could survive. The coincidence of sharing a unique spelling of my first name with a kid who lived in a town I had never heard of placed those fears right in my chest.

That personal connection spurred me to action. I e-mailed the story, along with an online petition, to everyone I knew and asked them to do the same. I posted the article on Facebook, started a MySpace group, and promoted them relentlessly on every message board I frequented. I sent e-mails to the Southern Poverty Law Center, American Civil Liberties Union, Urban League, NAACP, and Oprah, hoping to put the Jena Six on their radar. Time was of the essence, as Bell's sentencing was only a few months away.

I was one of many with the same idea. Everyday, the number of Facebook groups devoted to raising awareness grew from a handful to dozens, the number of signatures on the online petition increased by hundreds, then thousands. Nationally syndicated black radio shows started making the Jena Six case a part of their regular coverage, and the public outcry pushed "mainstream" media outlets like CNN to take notice. Al Sharpton got involved.

Day after day, this was all I found myself focusing on, and I told my *Script* team as much. My vision became clear, even if it didn't translate perfectly for the sports section: I was going to use all the resources available to me as editor in chief to help bring about justice for the Jena Six.

I envisioned stories about the case on every page, every week. I saw us sponsoring a student trip down to Jena to be a part of the protest that organizers were planning for the day Mychal Bell was to be sentenced. I imagined us hosting forums on campus about racial profiling, incarceration, and discriminatory policing.

I had big plans until I didn't. The gap between vision and reality is filled with unknowable obstacles. I hadn't counted on Hampton University standing in my way.

My entire rationale for attending an HBCU rested on the idea of them grooming me to be a Black Leader, which I saw as an outspoken, provocative, radical political figure in the tradition of Malcolm X and Huey P. Newton. I projected my mission onto Hampton without giving much thought to the fact that their most famous alumnus was Booker T. Washington, whose most famous address argued explicitly against black political activism. "It is at the bottom of life we must begin, and not at the top," he said. "Nor should we permit our grievances to overshadow our opportunities." Washington's accommodationist legacy of deemphasizing the fight for political equality in favor of "real estate or industrial skill" wasn't something I'd engaged. I didn't know he had learned from a paternalistic racist.

There was a strong sense of family at Hampton. That's true across HBCUs, and it's part of the reason young black students still choose them. What's the use of an education if you aren't cared for as a person? A living, breathing, feeling human being? When so many of us were still the first in our family to go off into the isolated world of higher education, it was comforting to walk into the cafeteria daily and hear "Sweetie, what you like?" It felt good to have professors like Professor Foster who assumed the role of advocate in addition to educator.

But Hampton's role as surrogate family tended to show up in that condescending paternalism that made you want to get away from home in the first place. The freshman curfew and gender-segregated dorms reflected an old-school approach to policing young people's "undesirable" behavior. The rule about business school students not being allowed to wear their hair in Afros or dreadlocks was pure assimilationist and seemed like it was written by the generation that still believed black hairstyles weren't "presentable." But disciplining a group of students for attempting to organize an Iraq War protest (this predated my time there) sent an explicit message: we're training you to go be a part of the

world, not to challenge it. Rebellion was treated as an arti-
fact of a history Hampton would rather teach than revive.

It was Booker T.'s legacy passed down, remixed, and required to wear a dark blue or black suit to official meetings.
And it's this legacy that I hadn't considered when I got back
to campus in the fall expecting administrative support in our
fight for the Jena Six.

I confronted that legacy head-on when I sat down with
the *Script* business adviser (keeper of our money) and told
her that I wanted to sponsor a bus trip down to Jena for the
march on September 20. It was the quickest and sternest
"no" I had heard since I was a child asking for new Jordans.
Her reason was that the newspaper's funds were to be spent
exclusively on the needs of the newspaper and its staff members, and chartering a bus for any student to board to Louisiana didn't fit the criteria. In hindsight, it's a perfectly
reasonable policy. My only argument was that at any time,
any student could be a staff member. You didn't have to apply to be able to write or edit for us. If you showed up to
meetings and took assignments at any point during the year,
you were staff. More to the bigger issue, I didn't understand
why she wouldn't stand behind me as we attempted to stand
behind the Jena Six. If ever there was a time to throw out the
rules, this seemed to be it.

But I resigned myself to disappointment on that front
and focused on the thing we could do, which was write about
the case relentlessly. I wanted the Jena Six on every page of
the paper. People needed to feel the urgency, the injustice,

the rage, whether they were reading the Local & World or Sports section. In the Campus section, we were being helped out by the fact that the fraternities Alpha Phi Alpha and Iota Phi Theta were organizing a rally to take place on September 20. HBCUs across the country were going to host rallies on their respective campuses that day, in solidarity with the planned march in Jena. I was proud to know my school would be among them.

Until we weren't. Booker T.'s legacy was always lurking. The Alphas and Iotas chose to host the rally in the student center from 12 p.m. to 2 p.m., which was usually a time reserved for a DJ to play music and students to congregate for midday partying and bullshitting. It made sense; rather than attempting to draw a large crowd for a political rally, they wanted to seize the one that was already there and shift their attention. The fraternities went through all the necessary steps to have the rally sanctioned by Student Activities and the dean of students, who offered his enthusiastic support of these young men choosing activism over apathy. Until he didn't. Two days before the rally, he revoked the permission he had just given the fraternities to rally at that time and place.

The reason offered by the dean was that a pep rally for the football game that would be taking place on campus that night was already scheduled for that exact time and that exact place. The Alphas and Iotas would need to move the time of the Jena Six rally to 5 p.m. in order to accommodate the pep rally. After some negotiation, the dean and the fraternities agreed that the Jena Six rally would take place during the first fifteen minutes of the original 12 to 2 timeslot, followed by the football team's pep rally.

Our Campus editor, a member of Alpha Phi Alpha, came into our offices, several of his frat brothers in tow, and related this story to the staff as we were working on putting together our first issue. All the pride I had evaporated and was replaced by the same rage I had felt when the Marines tried to recruit me and when I first read Mychal Bell's name. Except this time, the targets for my anger were supposed to be my allies. They were supposed to be my family.

For three years, I had sat in classrooms with professors who wondered aloud about why our generation was so apathetic, why we weren't activist-minded, why we hadn't continued the fight of our grandparents' generation. The 1960s are for Black America what the 1940s are for the whole of the country. Even the people who didn't live through that time mythologize the era as one of perfect nobility and virtue. Each subsequent generation lives in the shadow of comparison to "the Greatest Generation." At seventeen, eighteen, nineteen, twenty, I'd heard all about how my generation was not honoring the sacrifices made by the folks who faced down the police, and water hoses, and dogs, and left their blood in the streets hoping for freedom. We were squandering the opportunities they fought and died for, choosing only to think of ourselves and not the uplift of our communities.

For much of my life I had bought into this line of thinking. And I found myself surprised when so much energy was poured into getting justice for the Jena Six from my peers, the same people I'd looked down on when I got to Hampton's campus, assuming they didn't know Malcolm like I knew Malcolm, didn't know Huey like I knew Huey. I thought the fight gene had skipped an entire generation of black people, and by accident of birth I'd been caught in that time.

But what I felt when I heard what the dean told the Alphas and Iotas was different. We, as a generation, were standing up. We, as a generation, were ready to take on this fight. We, as a generation, were being told to fall back. If we, as a generation, were apathetic it was because our apathy was taught to us.

This split didn't cut clearly along generational lines, though, as evidenced by the fact that other HBCUs were able to get their rallies off the ground with full administrative support. It was ideological, Booker T.'s legacy made real for the twenty-first century. Standing in the student center, watching that truncated rally limp along, to be immediately followed by the cheerleading squad screaming "SHAKE IT, SHAKE IT, SHAKE DEEEEEEEZ NUTS!," was to live the natural result of that ideological legacy, where the potency of black political activism is undercut by the unfounded belief that we can find a place within the system and thrive. I was visibly mad.

But that anger was useless if I wasn't going to put any action behind it. It was already established that we would run a story about the way in which the situation played out, and Leslie (who'd served as chief copy editor of the *Script* the year before and had been co–Campus editor before stepping down to focus more on her physics requirements) was at work reporting and writing. There was a question that needed answering: If the pep rally had been planned all along, why approve the Jena Six rally in the first place?

It could have been a simple mistake, a double booking, an accident of bureaucracy. But that's not what Leslie's reporting found. She spoke with the dean of students, the director of student activities, the head coach of the football team, and several students involved in the planning of the rally. At the end of it all, she had been shown the student activities calendar, which the pep rally presumably would have appeared on had it been planned. But it wasn't, and wouldn't be until the director of student activities supplied her with a revised copy of the calendar with the pep rally written into the box for September 20, by hand. What's more, the football coach told her that they never do pep rallies on the day of a game, as it was generally seen as a distraction for the team. The dean of students continued to say he fully supported students' rights to express themselves politically, but this particular event conflicted with one that had been in the works.

Nothing added up. The pep rally, which would have had no involvement from the football team and didn't appear on the student activities calendar, was planned months in advance, but permission was still given to host the Jena Six rally for the same time and place? It didn't make sense and only further angered me. A front-page story that exposed the contradictions in the administration's story wasn't going to be enough.

I thought the issue was very clear: Hampton University, ever image-conscious, saw that news cameras were going to be on campus to cover the rally and didn't want to project to the world that its students were involved in anything resembling radical political action. They then revoked the permission for the rally in order to preserve their carefully curated image.

These are things I felt, but couldn't prove, and therefore couldn't print in a news story. But I could write an editorial that laid out my thoughts and feelings, based on the facts we had.

At the time, I still did my first and second drafts by hand. I scribbled them while sitting on the passenger side of Leslie's car, getting her to decipher my chicken scratch and tell me if she thought it was any good. Her first reaction was "oh my God" laughter. Her second was that it needed to be longer. Her third was, "You sure you want to do this?"

I took my draft and typed it up in the office, bypassing the normal copy-editing process and putting it straight onto the page that had already been laid out. This was Friday, one day after the rally. We were behind our planned schedule of sending off to press that day, in part because Leslie's story needed more time, but also because we were college students who did nothing in a timely fashion. We were going to finish up and get the whole thing sent off Monday to meet our publication date of the following Wednesday.

On Monday, our two advisers looked over the pages that were completed before we sent the files to the printer. This included my editorial. One of the advisers, herself a Hampton alum, asked me, "Are you sure this is what you want to say?"

I'd already made up my mind. I'd sat with it all weekend. There was, for me, no turning back. This was the action. This was using my words to move people, to fight. I finalized all the pages and sent them off later that night.

On Wednesday, two thousand copies of our first issue showed up to the office, with Leslie's story covering the front page and my editorial placed in the middle of the Opinion page. My first sentence read: "Hampton University hates black people."

Leslie had worried that it sounded too much like Kanye's "George Bush doesn't care about black people" and that it might distract people from my point. I was actively courting the comparison.

My piece went on to describe, in less detail than Leslie's story, the series of events surrounding the Jena Six rally, and then I offered my opinion about Hampton's suppression of student voices, and their interest in the prestige that football could bring over the controversy of a political rally raising awareness about injustice. I said that "the soul of Ronald Reagan rests his head on [the dean's] office at night." Reagan was the most evil white man I could think of who hadn't owned slaves.

I remember going to Professor Foster's office and asking him if he had seen the paper, and him grinning that grin that simultaneously frustrated and delighted me. He had seen it, he had read it, he had enjoyed it, but he didn't make too much of it. "You've proven you got a pair," he said to me. "Now what?"

Truth was, I had no plan. I'd written the piece without a step two in mind. I just knew it needed to be out there. And I knew there would be backlash.

The *Script*'s former business adviser, who worked in public relations for the university, called me in for a meeting. She said she was concerned that I wasn't taking my role as editor in chief seriously. She wondered why there was so much focus on what went wrong in planning the rally and not the rally itself. She said Hampton University is an entity made up of administrators, professors, alumni, and students, and asked who I was talking about when I said "Hampton University hates black people."

In that room, I didn't have an answer. When I had written it, I conceived of Hampton University as its administration, and she made a valid point I couldn't refute. Hampton University was more than a dean of students who callously revoked the permission for the rally, or the director of student activities who seemed to be lying about how long the pep rally had been planned. Hampton University was a 140-year-old institution that had produced black college graduates who had gone on to become mayors, comedians, authors, NBA players, educators, and the mother of Martin Luther King Jr. It became home and family for people seeking higher education who would have been denied the right to human dignity elsewhere. My rage hadn't allowed me to see that. If I had it to do all over again, I would have worded that sentiment very differently, without the Kanye allusion.

But the sentiment would remain the same. What I believed, and what I said in a haphazard way, was that standing in the way of young black people fighting against the injustice experienced by young black people in America is a method of destruction. They were not offering guidance, they were attempting to silence. I believed, as I do now, that attempting to muzzle the radical voices of young black people is not showing love. It's a disservice to our future and our freedom.

The source of my anger was that it was coming from my own people. I expected white people and white institutions to be committed to shutting me up. But the reality is that in order to exist with an endowment as large as Hampton's, you can't be seen as a threat. In order to ensure their survival, black institutions often dance the dance of capitulating to white supremacy, encouraging the silence that allows them to see another day.

But in time of crisis, our institutions have to be invested in more than their own survival. The Jena Six, to me, represented that crisis. Some people at Hampton didn't see it that way.

I wonder sometimes if that had to with who the Jena Six were, or who they weren't. A few of them had juvenile records. And they weren't innocent boys who were caught at the wrong place at the wrong time and just happened to fit the profile. They had actually jumped their classmate. Additionally, much of the original reporting that prompted the anger, connecting this fight to the nooses and a "white tree," later proved unreliable. In 2011, Stanford Law School professor Richard Ford told NPR's Michel Martin that "the Jena 6 protests were focused on a bad example of a real problem."

The real problem remains the way America's so-called criminal justice system thrives on taking black people away from their communities and locking them up. The real problem has been the ways "tough on crime" and "zero tolerance" have translated to more arrests and longer prison sentences. It is a problem that black children at younger and younger ages have come into contact with police and the "criminal justice system." But Ford was wrong in suggesting the Jena Six were a bad example of these problems.

For public relations purposes, it would be ideal if every victim of injustice was a person of unimpeachable character. If everyone was caught at the wrong place at the wrong time and was a rebuke to racist descriptors, half the work of reclaiming the victim's humanity would already be done. But the system isn't filled with a bunch of doe-eyed innocents, and that doesn't make them any less worthy of justice. They shouldn't be discarded as people on the basis of their mistakes.

My father once proudly told me that he had friends in prison whom he had never visited and never would. Friends he grew up with, experienced all the trial and error of youth alongside, but had made the kinds of mistakes (what kind, he would never say) that land a person in prison. He meant this as a cautionary tale about making the right choices in life, but I came away from it with the understanding that love was conditional and abandoning people who have been incarcerated is a righteous position.

The protests were never a matter of condoning the actions of the Jena Six, but rather a rejection of that line of thinking. We didn't need to believe that Robert Bailey, Carwin Jones, Bryant Purvis, Jesse Ray Beard, Theo Shaw, and Mychal Bell's actions were justified in order to believe they shouldn't be sent to prison for twenty-plus years. They were between the ages of fourteen and eighteen at the time of the fight, and had they served sentences similar to what Bell was originally facing, they would have been forty years old or approaching it when released, their young adulthoods taken from them, their second chances postponed until middle age with an accompanying felony record, based on an act of teenaged violence. Who would that benefit? Is that justice?

Thousands of us believed it wasn't. Thousands of us saw ourselves in the Jena Six. We felt the pain of destruction through the negligence of Hurricane Katrina, and mourned the cold-blooded killing of Sean Bell at the hands of police. The Jena Six tipped that frustration, sadness, and anger into action that would later be replicated in building a new movement for racial justice.

Because as much as the energy at the time felt like a movement was on the horizon, it lost steam and became a moment. An important moment, but it didn't congeal into the sort of generation-defining movement that came together after George Zimmerman killed Trayvon Martin.

Their cases were settled without much media fanfare. Bell's conviction was overturned on grounds that he was a minor being improperly charged as an adult, and upon retrial he pleaded guilty to reduced charges and had his time served count toward the eighteen-month sentence he received. The other five had their charges reduced, but it would be another two years before they each pled no contest to battery and received $500 fines and a week of probation. Ultimately, the protests were successful in the narrow scope of helping the Jena Six. What didn't happen, immediately, was addressing the overpolicing and criminalization of black youth or pushing a political agenda aimed at dismantling the systems that have rendered blackness illegal. It's not that everyone who had protested no longer cared, but how best to pursue that agenda wasn't entirely clear to us.

As far back as I can remember, every black elder in my life shared with me the same political message, in almost the same words: you have to vote because people died for your right to do so. Not because voting was the key to political power, or was a way to ensure representation within the system, but as recompense to the ancestors who saw voting as a pathway to freedom and fought to ensure it as a right. Of all the reasons for voting, this was always the least convincing to me. Obvious guilt trips annoy me, but no one had ever explained how voting was supposed to solve anything when all of my options resembled George W. Bush and John Kerry.

I wasn't the only one who received this messaging, but I was an outlier in the way I received it. In 2008, 55 percent of black eighteen-to-twenty-four-year-olds voted, an increase of 8 percent from the previous presidential election year. But it was more than just a sense of duty to the deceased that drove young black people to the polls. There's a reason *Ad Age* named Barack Obama their marketer of the year in 2008: he effectively sold hope better than anyone, and to an eager public. With 9/11, the Iraq War, Hurricane Katrina, the killing of Sean Bell, the Jena Six, and the task of entering true adulthood during the nation's worst economic downturn since the Great Depression weighing on us, hope was exactly what so many of us needed.

But Obama's brand of hope came at a price. Electoral politics is not activism. Winning votes and changing people's minds about deeply held beliefs would seem to be similar endeavors, but the former is less about selling ideas than it is selling a candidate. And when you commit to selling a candidate, compromise is key. You need to appeal to the broadest swath of people as possible.

The compromise that needed to be made in order to help sell Obama was to not mention the Jena Six. Or criminalizing black youth. Or blackness more generally. Obama needed to be Michael Jordan: amazing and black without reminding anyone he was black. He had to run to become president of the United States, not president of Black America. His supporters had to understand this and do their part in the selling. The young, black, college-educated people who were at the forefront of the protests for the Jena Six and who later became Obama volunteers and voters turned their attention from racial justice activism to electing the first black president. Those are two different things, and only one results in a movement. But in Obama, there was hope.

By the time George Zimmerman killed Trayvon Martin, the hope Obama sold had dissipated. His election was never seen, by any rational person, as a solution to American racism. But we were supposed to be able to celebrate hope, change, and progress. And we did, until Oscar Grant was killed nineteen days before Obama took the oath of office. And until Harvard historian Henry Louis Gates was arrested in front of his own home. And until Congressman Joe Wilson yelled "You lie!" at the first black president. And until the tea partiers depicted the first black president as a witch doctor. And until the first black president had to produce his long-form birth certificate to prove he was a citizen. Hope is too fragile an idea to withstand such an onslaught.

And the hope finally broke when George Zimmerman pulled the trigger and shot Trayvon Martin in his chest. Hope was no longer sufficient. Anger returned.

And as with the Jena Six, social media became the primary outlet for expressing that anger. Weeks went by before Zimmerman was arrested for killing Trayvon, and the only news source with regular coverage of the situation was Twitter. The cable news stations and major newspapers picked up the story only after the outrage at their negligence reached a fever pitch online. And while the legacy civil rights organizations dragged their feet, rallies and vigils were being planned in 140 characters or less. The Internet became the new grassroots.

The social media approach to activism that was in its infancy with the Jena Six was refined after George Zimmerman killed Trayvon Martin. At times, it has been derisively referred to as "slacktivism," the idea being that it requires no effort on the part of would-be activists to show their support. You no longer have to sacrifice in order to feel like you're helping the cause. All anyone had to do was change their social media profile picture to them wearing a hoodie, or put #Justice4Trayvon in a status update, and suddenly they were the movement. Our grandparents risked life and limb in the streets, were beaten by police officers and other defenders of white supremacy. We just clicked "like" on Facebook.

But that overlooks how powerful the image of people wearing their hoodies in solidarity could be. And that not everyone is physically capable of marching and protesting. And that social media is not meant as a replacement for direct action and civil disobedience. And that without social media, we likely would have never heard of Trayvon Martin in the first place. Without Twitter, news of Michael Brown's body lying in the street decaying because Officer Darren Wilson killed him and the police couldn't be bothered to move him wouldn't have penetrated outside of Ferguson for days, weeks, or ever. Twitter made it easier to make the invisible men visible.

"I am a man of substance, of flesh and bone, fiber and liquids—and I might even be said to possess a mind. I am invisible, understand, simply because people refuse to see me. . . . When they approach me they see only my surroundings, themselves, or figments of their imagination—indeed, everything and anything except me," Ralph Ellison wrote. Through social media, the substance of our existence was made real for the rest of the world.

I was something like a working writer when George Zimmerman killed Trayvon Martin. Freelancing is not steady, and in the era of $50–100 Internet pieces it is almost impossible to maintain financially. I was buoyed by the fact that I lived at home, a part of the wave of millennials who did the same postcollege.

I sat with Trayvon's death close to two weeks before deciding to write about it. He was killed the day before what would have been my cousin Demetri's thirtieth birthday, had he not been killed at age seventeen—the same age as Trayvon. I was trying to protect my fragile sanity, only tuning in to the Twitter outrage in spurts. But the longer Zimmerman was allowed to walk free, and the longer it took for national media outlets to pay attention, the more the weight of responsibility fell on me. I owed it to the "flesh and bone, fiber and liquids" who Zimmerman had seen as no more than a "figment of his imagination" to be his voice.

I'd given up on the idea of becoming a Black Leader. The pressure was never good for my anxiety, and I had started to realize that the entire concept reeked of elitism and self-aggrandizement. Why that had never occurred to me before is part of the seduction. But I could be what Baldwin said—"an honest man and a good writer"—in service of my people. Toward the end of my run as editor in chief of the *Hampton Script*, our former business adviser told me I couldn't be a good journalist because I was an activist. I don't know if she meant it as an insult, but I embraced this. Being a journalist was never something I aspired to, but rather fell into accidentally. Not being a good one didn't bother me. If being an activist meant that I was approaching my work not as an observer but as an advocate, not as a curious outsider but as an active participant in struggle, then so be it. Honest and good. For my people. For Trayvon.

I pitched his story to one outlet, and after several unanswered e-mails, they finally said no. The Twitter outcry for media attention hadn't yet reached the editors of major publications. But I thought the *Nation* might go for it. Since being introduced to it my third year of college (I'd been assigned *Democracy NOW!* and the *Nation* in one of my sociology courses, and also Jeremy Scahill's *Blackwater* was all over the place), I'd known it to be a magazine willing to stand with the people on the margins. One of their editors, Liliana Segura, followed me on Twitter, and on a whim I sent her a series of direct messages explaining what happened to

Trayvon and what I wanted to write. I was surprised a day later when she told me yes and that I needed to e-mail her. I started writing shortly after that.

While working on edits, the 911 tape that caught audio of Trayvon's last moments was released. Listening to it was the first time I allowed myself tears. George Zimmerman killed his "flesh and bone, fiber and liquids" and made it so we never got to know his mind. And here it was, the act preserved for posterity. I felt sick. I'd wanted to write for the *Nation* for some time, and here was my opportunity, but at what cost? I felt like I was exploiting Trayvon's death, the mourning of his family and friends, for my own career advancement. No matter that my heart was in the right place; I'd be receiving a paycheck and national platform to speak about the death of someone I never saw.

When I turned in the final piece, I remembered reading about how the late historian Manning Marable's first assignment as a journalist was covering Martin Luther King Jr.'s funeral. To be a writer is to bear witness; to be a black writer is to bear witness to tragedy. In order to be honest and good, this is something I can't escape.

That job—bearing witness—is often at odds with my other job—as a black man—which is to survive by any means necessary. Honestly bearing witness requires writing about things that could easily put your life in danger. To write about Trayvon Martin was not just to write about George Zimmerman shooting and killing him. It was bigger than that single act. To write about Trayvon Martin was to indict a history, a system, a country that made George Zimmerman possible. He didn't spring forth from the womb seeing young black men in hoodies as assholes that always get away. America taught him that. To write about Trayvon Martin was not just about expressing sympathy to his family, but dealing with how America created the nigger.

The nigger is America's greatest asset and its biggest fear. The nigger represents the bottom, from slavery to incarceration, America's most reliable source of exploited labor. The nigger generates profit that America feels no obligation to share. The nigger is reminded of its position at the bottom by being shuttered off in the worst neighborhoods with the least amount of resources, while being told to be grateful for America's benevolence. And so long as the nigger exists, America can say to its other exploited populations, "At least you aren't the nigger."

But every now and then, some of America's niggers get it in their heads that they deserve the right to walk free in the world. They start believing they are worthy of being treated like humans, with dignity and compassion. But if every one of America's niggers started believing this—America's greatest fear—and demanded as much, America as we know it would cease to exist. America ain't America without its nigger. So from time to time, America needs to send a message to its niggers that being a nigger is the safe bet—that it's actually better to be a nigger than to live free. And America, impetuous adolescent of a country that it is, sends this message through violence.

More often than not, the violence is slow and undetectable to those who aren't niggers. The niggers go to dilapidated schools. The niggers don't get tested for certain diseases when they go to the doctor. The niggers breathe the most polluted air. The niggers work longer hours at more strenuous jobs for less money. But sometimes the violence is more direct. Sometimes a George Zimmerman kills a Trayvon Martin.

Bearing witness, as an honest black man and good black writer, means saying as much. And saying it over and over, because America keeps killing its niggers, over and over. It is recognizing that America does not hate us, but that it killed Sean Bell, Oscar Grant, Ramarley Graham, Jordan Davis, and Freddie Gray to remind us of our place.

Michael Brown wasn't killed because of hate. America would prefer he still be alive, still flesh and bone, fiber and liquids to exploit. But he passed into territory where he made himself not only seen but dangerous to America's sense of self. Walking down the street and refusing to accept the limitations of the nigger's place, he became what America fears. He became a threat. Acting on behalf of America, Officer Darren Wilson eliminated the threat. Michael Brown was a sacrifice, one made millions of times over by America, to ensure that the rest of its niggers stay in line. That's why his body lay there, bleeding out onto the pavement of Canfield Drive, for four and a half hours. Not because of neglect, but because it was a message: Here is your punishment. Here is what happens to American niggers who don't stay in their place. And that message creates a desire in the rest of us niggers for the relative safety offered by choosing the invisibility that comes along with being a cog or killer.

A few months after George Zimmerman killed Trayvon Martin, I got my third tattoo. On my left bicep, I put "Invisible man, got the whole world watching . . . ," a lyric from Mos Def's "Hip Hop." I'd wanted to do it for a while, and the timing, sadly, felt right. In the song, Mos is speaking specifically to the idea of hip-hop's global popularity bringing unfounded attention on the invisible man Ellison had eloquently described. He charts black men's rise through labor, music, and commerce in the preceding lines: "We went from picking cotton / to chain gang line chopping / to be-bopping / to hip-hopping / blues people got the blue chip stock option."

But "Invisible man, got the whole world watching" came back to me after Trayvon's death with new meaning and questions. The challenge of overcoming invisibility is one that black men take up daily in the quest to live freely as ourselves. And in some rare instances, we can make the world stand up and pay attention—to extend to us basic humanity for the price of either our sanity or integrity. But Trayvon Martin and Jordan Davis and Michael Brown and Oscar Grant didn't choose their visibility—it was thrust upon them by the same system that made them invisible to begin with. In death, they came into full view as flesh and blood, fiber and liquids, minds, hearts, and souls. The price for their humanity was their lives. As black men, must we always choose? Can we not live free, with our humanity, sanity, and integrity intact, even as the world watches? Are we destined to forever be the Invisible Man?

"Invisible to whom?" Toni Morrison has asked. Growing up, I'd heard nothing but praise for Ellison's novel, and I came to swear by its wisdom when I finally read it during my second summer in Atlanta. Morrison's question, one I didn't hear until watching her in a late-2013 conversation with novelist Junot Díaz, had never crossed my mind, but it's the most important question to consider while reading *Invisible Man*. When Ellison wrote, "I am invisible, understand, simply because people refuse to see me," "people" didn't mean every person alive across the globe—it meant white people. Invisibility is established through white people's refusal to see black men as fully human. In one sense, ceding this much power to the white gaze makes sense, as the world we inhabit is dominated by the economy, government, and culture that imbues whiteness with every conceivable benefit. Being invisible to these systems has real material consequences.

But it's Morrison's response to her own question—"Not me"—that reveals the novel's greatest flaw: Ellison's focus on visibility vis-à-vis whiteness and white people makes invisible the very people who are able to see him—black women.

A year after Darren Wilson killed Michael Brown, I traveled to Ferguson to be a part of a weekend of commemoration. It was only my second time in Ferguson, having gone in November, right before the announcement that Wilson would not be indicted on any charges related to shooting and killing Brown. The atmosphere then was, understandably, much more tense than when I returned. The anniversary weekend was a time of reflection and, in some ways, celebration. Not of the tragedy that took Michael Brown's life, but of the spirit of resistance it had encouraged in the young people who had, one year earlier, decided they would no longer allow the fear of police violence to control their lives.

There were so many young people out in the streets— twenty-somethings on down to babies born in the interim year. Whether or not the new movement produced any substantial policy changes felt secondary in those moments, as I heard five- and six-year-old marchers chant along that "black lives matter." What they would know, regardless of the political outcome of the movement, was that someone thought their black life mattered. Thousands of people had come to their hometown to stand with them and assert their right to live free. That is a revolution in itself.

But mostly boys. The younger ones running through the streets with their shirts off, some of the older ones cliqued up and cracking jokes. Those boys were receiving the message (no matter how much organizers attempted to include black women who were victims of state violence) that their lives matter, and that when those lives are being threatened someone will stand up for them. Not just "someone," though. Black women.

Black women have always been on the front lines and behind the scenes of the fight for racial justice in America.

There's nothing revelatory in that statement. There's also nothing revelatory in noting that racial justice movements have tended to focus on black men's experiences, or that they retroactively become tales of charismatic black male leadership uplifting the masses and guiding them through the darkness. This is the sort of erasure that black feminists have constantly pushed back against. What hasn't been settled is how to produce a shift.

Because when twenty-two-year-old Rekia Boyd was shot and killed by an off-duty Chicago police detective on March 21, 2012, the streets didn't erupt in fury. Vigils didn't spring up across the country in honor of nineteen-year-old Renisha McBride, shot and killed in Dearborn Heights, Michigan, while seeking help after crashing her car on November 2, 2013. There was no wall-to-wall cable news coverage or burning of any CVS stores after the Detroit Police Department's Special Response Team invaded the wrong home and shot a sleeping seven-year-old, Aiyana Stanley-Jones, on May 16, 2010. Their names and stories reached and remain in our collective consciousness only because social media, Twitter in particular, ensured that they wouldn't be forgotten.

And I'm not being an honest black man and a good black writer by simply saying "social media" or "Twitter." Even the official-unofficial tag "Black Twitter" is incomplete. It was black women on Twitter who pushed us all to pay attention to the stories of Rekia, Renisha, Aiyana—and Trayvon, Jordan, Michael, and all the rest. It was black women organizing the early vigils and protests while the Sanford Police

Department couldn't decide if shooting an unarmed teen-ager warranted an arrest under the laws they had sworn to uphold. It was black women who claimed the streets as their own and led the marches and protests against police vio-lence. It was black women who nursed the wounds from rubber bullets and cared for those who had breathed in tear gas. It was black women who fed the tired protestors, gave them safe houses to sleep in, and prayed for them.

While running through the streets a year after Michael Brown's death, shirtless and carefree, learning to love and value themselves, were these black boys also learning to love and value the black women fighting to keep their black asses alive?

I thought about Leslie. How I wouldn't have known about the Jena Six without her. How she listened through my anger. How she coaxed my doubts about being able to step into the role of editor in chief. How she stepped up to write our biggest story. How I leaned on her to reassure me that it was okay to say "Hampton University hates black people." How, in the months that followed, my campus ac-tivism kicked up and I'd come by her dorm room late at night and lay all my worries on her while she stood in the doorway, attentive and affectionate. And how I repaid her by never saying "I love you."

I reaped the benefits of her emotional and intellectual labor without ever asking how I could support her. I barely said "thank you." She was there, making time for me, making time for a black boy in Louisiana who shared my name, through her tough schedule and pressure to maintain straight As and all her postgraduation concerns and my emotional distance. She was there. She saw me. It fills me with deep regret that I'm unable to say the same.

But such is the story of black women standing behind and by black men through the most challenging parts of our existence, and black men looking behind and beside ourselves and not seeing black women standing there.

We don't even have to ask black women to sacrifice for our survival; they do so without formal request. In turn, we dismiss the concerns of black womanhood as trivial or divisive, failing to see black women's pain as real or in need of our attention.

We rallied for the Jena Six, but we don't speak to the ways in which black girls have their voices and behaviors policed in school settings. We balk at the number of black men locked behind prison walls while ignoring the increasing number of black women with similar fates. We recognize the detrimental effects the War on Drugs has had on black men and our interactions with the police, but there's no similar discussion about the ways the criminalization of sex work is a pretense for police harassment of black women, black trans women in particular.

This is not accidental. We haven't been neglecting black women as substance, of flesh and bone, fiber and liquids—and minds—through some collective black male brain fart. We have done so because we have come to believe in patriarchy and male dominance as the realization of freedom.

The black liberation fights from our history that we remember so fondly were about the economic and political empowerment of black men, which would allow us to take our place as the heads of our homes, able to provide for and protect our wives and children. Even the Montgomery Bus Boycott, rooted in the sexual assault faced by black women on public transportation, somehow morphed into this fight to restore dignity to black manhood.

As the 1980s and '90s gave way to the "endangered species" narrative with regard to young black men, we mourned for the loss of life, but even more so for the loss of potential patriarchs who wouldn't be around to teach boys "how to be men" or girls how a "real man" should treat them. We pretended they would know. We ignored that they learned those lessons from other broken men. What's more, we pretended that this would be salvation. That subjecting black families to the wills and whims of black men would make white supremacy crumble.

So we poured all of our intellectual and activist energy into saving black men. In the process, we haven't just ignored the way that white supremacy killed Rekia and Renisha and Aiyana, and all the other names we refused to learn: we have excused the violence black women face from black men.

"Many of us are fearful of the same men who organize alongside us for black liberation," Ashley Yates, a St. Louis–area activist who gained notoriety after the killing of Michael Brown, told Mic.com. "Men with power in the movement. Men who have done great work towards black liberation. We have been silenced, shamed, assaulted and raped by these very men. We wonder if anyone besides us can hold those competing truths simultaneously."

Yates expressed the concerns of generations of black women who have stood on the front lines for black liberation, only to go home and have to fight for their own private salvation. The other side of restoring dignity to black manhood through patriarchy and male dominance is where that dignity is derived—the subjugation of black women. We have used the same violence America used to turn us into niggers, and remind us we are niggers, against black women, and then we asked for their loyalty. And against the logic of self-preservation, they have given it to us. We use our anger at the state as a justification for the violence we enact on black women, then tell them not to hold us accountable until we have defeated racism. Those carefree, shirtless, joyful black boys in Ferguson could grow up thinking this is how revolution works.

Unless we recognize that liberation for black men based in patriarchy and male dominance is liberation for no one, least of all black women, but not for black men either. It turns us into the very oppressors we claim to be fighting against. It makes us deny parts of ourselves in service of an idea of masculinity that does more to destroy than build.

Recognition is only a first step. Recognition is the easy part. The work of unlearning patriarchy requires an intense self-interrogation, which means getting beyond the self-congratulation and complacency of acknowledging patriarchy's existence. It's not just answering Toni Morrison's question; it's asking more questions of ourselves.

Because divesting from a system of oppression that has given us an identity, a way to see ourselves, isn't easy. Change is hard, and building a world of true justice and equality will require us to become new. Change is not inevitable, and building a world of true justice and equality will not happen if we don't commit to building those new selves.

Complacency is easy, and when we aren't the Chris Browns and Bill Cosbys of the world, it's hard to see why change is necessary. But we have to ask ourselves: Is that enough? Is it enough to not beat a woman unrecognizable? Is it enough to not drug and rape dozens of women? Is that the bar we want to set for our humanity?

Because even when we aren't the Chris Browns or Bill Cosbys, we still destroy. There isn't a man alive who hasn't abused a woman in some way. Through outright lies and lies of omission, deception and manipulation, exploitation and judgment, silencing and ignoring. We do this in realms political, economic, social, sexual, professional, and in whatever spaces they may meet.

These aren't gendered behaviors, but they take on a different resonance when it is men doing the lying, manipulating, judging, and silencing within the confines of a patriarchal system. It's another layer of destruction when it is black men doing the omitting, deceiving, exploiting, and ignoring of black women who have always fought for them.

None of us is exempt, even those of us who read bell hooks and claim to know better. None of us has done enough work to unlearn patriarchy and male dominance, to open ourselves up to true equality and justice, to build new selves. Because none of us has done enough to see the black women standing right there, nursing our wounds and holding the truth of their oppression.

It is not beyond us to do so. We fail to understand black womanhood only because we refuse to try. It is not only possible, it is necessary. We can answer Toni Morrison's question, and when we do, we'll find the parts of ourselves we have buried.

Chapter 5

On May 17, 2013, thirty-two-year-old Mark Carson was shot in the face in the Greenwich Village neighborhood of New York City. He and a friend were confronted by three men, one of whom said to them, "Look at these faggots," and "What are you, gay wrestlers?" The groups exchanged words before Carson and his friend decided it was best they walk away, but the three men followed them, yelling things like "faggot" and "queer" in their direction. One of them, Elliot Morales, pulled out a gun and, while pointing it at the two men, said, "Do you want to die right now?," to which Carson replied, "Do you want to shoot us in front of all these people?" Morales then shot Carson and ran away. Mark Carson was taken to local Beth Israel Hospital where he was pronounced dead.

"I thought that kind of hate stuff was gone, but I see that it's not," Mark's father, Mark Carson Sr., said. "It's simply ridiculous. People are what people are. They do what they do. You can't knock down who people are."

Twenty-two-year-old Dionte Greene was also shot in the face. In the early hours of October 31, 2014, Greene, a Kansas City resident, had plans to meet a person with whom he'd had online correspondence—some "trade"—before attending a party. "Trade," according to *Guardian* writer Zach Stafford, is a term "used within black LGBT communities to describe a man who doesn't 'appear gay' but who engages in sex with men unbeknownst to his family and most of his friends. Trade is a man you don't necessarily trust—more of a risk than many are willing to take."

Greene sat in his car at the spot where he'd agreed to meet with this "trade," talking on the phone with a friend while waiting for the man to arrive. "He looks just like his Facebook picture," Greene told his friend on the other line as the man approached the car. Before the line went dead, Greene's friend heard yelling. Dionte was found dead later that morning.

"I wasn't so much against it," Coshelle Greene, Dionte's mother, told Stafford about how she felt when Dionte "came out" to her at age sixteen. "I just didn't want it for mine. I just knew how society looks at it, and how it's so frowned upon."

Mark Carson and Dionte Greene were killed in the same years where outrage over the deaths of Trayvon Martin, Jordan Davis, Michael Brown, John Crawford, Tamir Rice, Freddie Gray, and others fueled protests, uprisings, and new conversations about the dangers facing young black men in America. But their names are not included in that evergrowing tragic roll call. They don't make it onto the Helvetica font T-shirts, aren't part of the chants emanating from the streets; their hashtag funerals were sparsely attended. I didn't sit down to write a book because their deaths made me ask questions about my identity and place in the world.

Mark and Dionte were young, black, and male and should have fit the criteria for inclusion in the club of martyrdom. They were unarmed. They were targeted for their identities—or rather, the way in which their identities are read by the world—just as Trayvon, Jordan, Michael, John, Tamir, and Freddie were. They may not have been killed by police, but neither were Trayvon or Jordan. Not every unarmed black man who is shot and killed becomes a martyr and a cause, but among those who do, the other thing they have in common is that they're straight, or presumed to be so.

It's a curious, and rather insulting, thing we do. We know that there are multiple sexual identities, and yet we assume everyone is straight, unless explicitly stated otherwise or when we think we can tell by just looking. That's our societal default and most of us operate from there until given reason not to. And when we learn that a person doesn't fit the default assignation of sexual identity, we have to decide something almost instantly: Are they no longer worthy of my sympathy?

In the cases of Mark Carson and Dionte Greene, the answer seems clear: no. Around 1,500 people did show up for a rally in New York City after Carson's death, but his name receded from the headlines within days. Dionte barely made it on the radar beyond some coverage in local newspapers and a few LGBT-focused blogs.

The most prominent LGBT activism of recent years has focused on making marriage equality the law of the land, with the notable exception being Dan Savage's "It Gets Better" campaign, a response to a spate of suicides by young people who had faced vicious bullying for being gay. But the thought of being able to legally marry the person you love is a sweet, distant fantasy that has little effect on the increasing number of LGBT homeless youth and the violence that accompanies a life on the street. Telling young people who are being bullied for their (perceived or actual) sexual identity that "It Gets Better" provides a feel-good moment of encouragement but obscures the fact that, sometimes, it doesn't.

It didn't for Mark and Dionte. And who advocates for them? The mainstream LGBT movement poured so much of its energy into normalizing the "G" in LGBT through the campaigns for marriage equality and ending the military's "don't ask, don't tell" policy, you could almost be forgiven for having thought that antigay violence ended after the death of Matthew Shepard. And black gay men were not who was envisioned when black communities started to bemoan black men's condition as an "endangered species." We haven't developed a script for dealing with the violence inflicted upon them because we still haven't gotten to a place where we can fully see them.

We're very clear on seeing them as punch lines. I learned that as a kid before I knew what gay meant, whenever I managed to dodge my parents' control and catch an episode of *In Living Color* where Damon Wayans and David Alan

Grier did "Men on Films," their caricature of black gay men reviewing popular movies. It didn't take any understanding of sexuality to laugh at the idea that a man wanted to touch/hold/kiss another man, because visually they made it seem the height of abnormality. Their necks snapped, their hands limped, their lips pursed, their teeth sucked, their clothes—bright, feminine—appeared onscreen before they did. And they talked like when men made fun of women. I laughed the same childish laugh as everyone around me every time they said "Hated it!"

Then later I learned what gay meant, and subsequently learned it wasn't something you wanted to be. The playgrounds and basketball courts gave me the language. Anything and everything that was undesirable we called gay. The rules about when and how to take the ball out after a made shot were gay. The home base during tag was gay. Being assigned homework on the weekend was gay. The cafeteria not serving pizza was gay.

And any person suspected of being gay, we called a faggot. And then we laughed. And then the person being called a faggot got angry. And you didn't have to do much to be suspected. And you never really recovered from the charge, unless you could prove someone else was the faggot. And all of this made sense to us.

These were rules established in preadolescence, when we barely knew what sex was but were certain we had sexuality figured out. Of course, we didn't make these rules up ourselves; they were handed down to us from older siblings, big cousins, wise uncles, and rappers who felt like all three. Some of us picked it up from parents, but I didn't. Mine never discussed anything related to sex or sexuality around me. Until I was thirteen, the extent of my sex education was my parents telling me to cover my eyes whenever a sex scene came on during a movie we were watching together. And when my father finally did have "the talk" with me—the only conversation about sex we would ever have—he assumed.

I don't remember much of what he actually said after his initial question. "What do you know about sex?" I awkwardly gulped through an answer about there being sexually transmitted diseases, having no desire to have a conversation with my father about the mechanics of intercourse. But he managed to get the talk back where he wanted it, so he could recite the platitudes about waiting until you're ready, using condoms, and respecting women. I didn't walk away with any greater understanding of sex, only on a flush of embarrassment and the hope that this meant I would no longer have to cover my eyes during sex scenes.

I'm not sure how I would have reacted if he didn't approach the talk with the assumption I was straight. I wouldn't have been comfortable. Gay had come to mean something very specific and the accusations carried new consequences. In elementary and middle school there was teasing, but in high school there was the real potential for violence. If you were identified as gay, whether it was true or not, and either accidentally or purposefully touched another boy for any reason, you could end up on the receiving end of a punch in the face. Being touched by a gay dude and doing nothing about it meant you, too, must be gay. And this made sense to us.

But my father didn't make that assumption with my comfort in mind. Gay meant something specific to him, too, and it wasn't something he wanted his sons to be. I realized this in college. Spring break and the Oscars happened to coincide my sophomore year. It was the year *Brokeback Mountain* was unceremoniously robbed of the Best Picture award in favor of the faux-progressive racial politics of *Crash* (though I thought the most memorable moment was Three 6 Mafia winning an Oscar for "It's Hard Out Here for a Pimp"). The day after the award show, Oprah hosted a special show with winners and nominees from the Kodak Theatre. She was interviewing Ang Lee, who had won Best Director for *Brokeback Mountain*, adding to the controversy of it not winning Best Picture. My father and I had been watching Oprah's post-Oscar special together in relative silence until then. But he wanted to take our bonding to the next level.

"I grew up watching westerns," he said, "and in all my years of watching westerns, I never thought of cowboys being faggots."

I'd heard the word many, many times. I'd said it more than a few times. But hearing it come out of my father's mouth was the first time the word "faggot" made me bristle.

Things were different. It would be too generous to call me a reformed homophobe, because I still thought it was completely acceptable to mimic Dave Chappelle's singing white woman and sing "gay sex is gross," but politically, at least, I found homophobia reprehensible. But even that was less about embracing gay people's humanity than it was standing in opposition to the conservatives and Christians who had made denying gay people rights part of their agenda. I knew only that if they were for it I had to be against it, and vice versa. Gay rights had simply become one of the major issues of the day and I had chosen the side George Bush wasn't on.

With that tiny bit of reformed thinking, though, I felt a deep discomfort hearing my father say "faggot." He wouldn't curse or drink hard liquor in front of me, and though I was legally an adult by this time he still had a problem with my buying and listening to rap music, but calling people "faggots" was alright with him. I sat hoping to get back to the silence we had previously enjoyed, but when he repeated the slur ("You can't convince me John Wayne was playing a faggot," he said), I got up and left the room. My silent protest to his attempt at hetero-male bonding likely didn't sit well with him. He probably breathed a sigh of relief the next year when I brought Leslie home.

I shouldn't have been surprised, though, when he asked me with grave parental concern, "Is Justin gay?"

Anyone who has visited an HBCU campus for any length of time usually makes the same remark: "It's such a fashion show." This isn't a lie, and Hampton was no exception. Style was of as much importance as your GPA. But style took time to develop, particularly fitting that style to the Hampton aesthetic. As seventeen- and eighteen-year-old freshmen, we came to campus looking like seventeen- and eighteen-year-olds, which at the time meant looking like extras in a Juelz Santana video. Our pants were big, our white T-shirts long, and our sneakers had to match every color in the rest of our outfit. Over time, with our eyes toward adulthood and some toward corporate success, our pants shrank and we traded white tees for properly fitted polos. While we all transformed, some pushed the boundaries of fashion and style further than others.

Justin arrived to campus full formed. He's still the only man I know who was rocking Gucci sunglasses at eighteen without them looking tacky. But Justin wasn't just stylish for his own sake. He had his sights set on becoming a fashion designer. He was always sketching something, and every (actual) fashion show that Hampton held he designed and made original clothes for. I was asked more than a few times by our classmates if Justin was gay.

We'd met in the same place I'd met everyone who I was remotely close to on campus, in the *Script* office. He was the photo editor during our junior year. If I'd bought into every stereotype of gay men that I knew, I would have guessed that Justin was gay. He had a slightly feminine animation when he spoke excitedly, did that thing where he sucked his teeth and started a sentence with "Girl . . . ," always had a fresh manicure, was more interested in fashion than sports, and was a man obsessed with Beyoncé. But his, or anyone else's, sexuality was none of my concern. And my father's comment about "cowboys being faggots" had caused me to do some reflection on my own attitudes. I was doing my best to check my assumptions, if not my outright bigotry.

Justin lived in an off-campus apartment junior year all by himself. He constantly had people over because he was a social butterfly who didn't like being alone for too long. When I mentioned that I wanted to move off campus for senior year, we both thought it would be a good idea to move in together.

I was back in Atlanta for the summer, and laser focused on the Jena Six, which meant I wasn't going to be much help in the apartment hunt. So Justin met up with my father to look at some places. I trusted that whatever was good enough for Justin and his Gucci messenger bag would definitely be good enough for me.

When I got back home at the end of summer, all ready to move in, my father asked me, "Is Justin gay?" It wasn't just an inquiry. He said it in a hushed tone, the kind they employ in the movies when someone asks, "Are you sure you're innocent?"

"I don't know," I told him, because I honestly didn't. Did Justin have a girlfriend? No. Did Justin talk about once having a girlfriend? Yes. Did Justin fit some gay stereotypes? Yes. Did Justin ever say he was gay? No. And I never asked. I didn't care—or I was trying to convince myself that I didn't care.

"He seems like a nice guy, though," my father said, as if he had previously considered being gay and a nice guy to be incompatible characteristics that might be able to coexist in Justin if he were gay. I staged another silent protest and left the room.

I moved in with Justin the next week and found out he was gay. Not right away, but Brandon was over quite a bit in the first few weeks after we first moved in. Then he was over nearly every day. And Brandon's car would be outside when I left for class in the morning. Then he had a key.

Justin never "came out" to me, as awkward as that phrase is. One day he caught me as I was about to leave the apartment and said, "Brandon's going to start paying a third of the rent." I smiled and said, "Yeah, okay, sounds good." And that was that.

Brandon was the first man Justin had ever dated. I was happy for my friend. He was giving himself permission to be his full self. And I was happy I could self-righteously declare myself to not be a homophobe.

I lived with two gay men, how could I be homophobic? I was uncomfortable with the word "faggot," how could I be homophobic? I believed gay people should have the right to get married, how could I be homophobic? I'd watched *Brokeback Mountain* and didn't turn away once, how could I be homophobic?

One of the privileges of not being a part of a marginalized group is believing you can set your own benchmarks for bigotry. But I'd also made the mistake of defining homophobia—a term that suggests fear of homosexuality—as something external. I wasn't afraid of gay people, or of witnessing expressions of same-sex attraction. I was, however, afraid of someone believing I was gay.

The foundation of so much of hetero-male bonding is a reinforcing of the "hetero" part of your identity. You can accomplish this in a few ways, but one tried-and-true device is distancing yourself from any hint of same-sex attraction. This is why "no homo" and "pause" became popular phrases. If you ever said anything that could in any way be misconstrued as gay, you could follow up with "no homo" or "pause" to prove your heterosexuality.

Postcollege I would swear off "no homo" and "pause" altogether, declaring them childish and hateful. But in my high school and college years, even when I thought I was enlightened, I used "no homo" pretty regularly. But sometimes, I didn't need the phrase. One night, Justin and I threw a party at our apartment. All of our friends were over, and among Justin and Brandon's friends were a number of other gay men. When the party was over, I quietly remarked to someone, "There were way too many gay men in my apartment tonight."

And the thing is, I wasn't even uncomfortable with the number of gay men there. Or the fact that a couple of them had been caught having sex in Justin's bathroom. None of this bothered me. In the moment, I just felt compelled to bond with another straight dude and all the gay men were an easy target. Homophobia is a social lubricant for straight men.

But what do we gain from such deep insecurity about the perception of our sexuality? Or more importantly, what do we lose? We miss out on tenderness, on the opportunity to forge bonds with one another on the basis of openness and compassion. We qualify our greetings, compliments, and affections for one another to ensure they aren't read as sexual, and in the process cheapen them. And how much brainpower are we wasting by policing everything we say for the slightest sexual connotation?

At greater issue, though, is what all this says to gay men: You are not a part of the brotherhood. Your existence is not only illegitimate, it is a threat. If ever the threat becomes too much, it will be eliminated. Our fear should be yours.

On my third ever visit to New York City I was hit on by a man for the first time. It was spring of 2009 and "I want to be a writer" had turned into "I want to be a screenwriter" after several years of film snobbery and a summer spent writing the screenplay that kept me alive through severe depression and anxiety. On my first trip to New York, I'd met some filmmakers who'd invited me to come back and work on a short film they were completing. I jumped at the chance and onto the Amtrak they were paying for.

The day I arrived, the director asked me if I'd like to go with him to see a movie. A film called *Gomorrah* was playing at the IFC Center that he really wanted to see. It was an Italian mafia movie and Martin Scorsese was involved, so how could I turn it down? We would meet at the theater.

I got off the train, proud of myself for not getting terribly lost, and walked across the street to the IFC to purchase my ticket. I'd gotten there fairly early, afraid I would mess up the trains, so I stood outside waiting for my director friend to show up.

I knew nothing about New York City's neighborhoods. At that point, I'd only spent any significant amount of time in Harlem and Bed-Stuy. I couldn't explain the difference between SoHo, Morningside Heights, or Midtown, much less point them out on a map. When my director friend arrived he told me we were in the West Village. Before he got there, I learned the West Village had many popular gay hangouts.

Standing there waiting, I saw more gay men than I'd probably ever seen in my life. And that wasn't my being presumptuous based on gay stereotypes. This was based on the evidence of hand-holding, making out, and loud, proud proclamations. I let out a few less-than-enlightened WOWs that no one else could hear.

After waiting for a while, I walked up a block or two to see if maybe I was standing in the wrong place, that perhaps my director friend was somewhere else waiting for me. But I didn't see him anywhere nearby, so I decided to turn around and reclaim my spot in front of the theater. While I was walking back, I passed a man wearing a black turtleneck, black leather jacket, and black kufi who turned around and followed me. I didn't think he was following me until I stopped and he was standing there right next to me. "Hi, how are you doing?" he asked. Without thinking I responded, "I'm fine." In an instant I regretted it, worried that I'd just engaged in my first conversation with a crazy New Yorker.

"You going to the movies?"

"Yeah."

"What movie are you going to see?"

I turned and gestured toward the poster.

"Oh, Martin Scorsese, he makes a lot of gangster movies."

"Yeah," I said, thinking *No shit, Sherlock,* and politely smiled and nodded.

"You meeting someone here?"

"Yeah, I'm waiting on someone."

"Oh okay. . . . Maybe you and me could go to the movies one day."

It still hadn't dawned on me what was happening. He was still just a crazy New Yorker to me. I smiled awkwardly and said, "No, that's aight."

"No, I'm not your type?"

Now it was clear. And now I didn't know how to handle this. So I continued smiling awkwardly. "Nah."

"What kind of guys do you like?"

"Oh . . . women."

He flinched. "Oh, you like women? I'm sorry, I didn't meant to offend you . . ." and he took a few steps back. There was a whole new look on his face.

I'm about five eight and at that time around 135 pounds, but you would have guessed less by looking at me. Physically imposing is something I've never been. This man was six-feet tall and from the looks of it kept a pretty decent gym regimen. If ever there was a reason for us to fight, all the smart money would be on him. But right then, he was afraid of me.

"No no, it's okay, it's okay, I'm not offended," I tried to convince him, tried to soften my face and tone, tried to put him back at ease.

"Okay, okay. Again, I'm sorry. Enjoy your movie." We shook hands and he walked away. When my director friend arrived, I relayed the whole experience to him, and then to anyone else who would listen for the rest of the time I was in New York.

Approaching strangers in any setting has never been something my perpetually shy self has done often, and even less so when it comes to women I'm attracted to. I wouldn't know where to begin a conversation. But the worst scenarios I could ever imagine involved embarrassment and rejection. A man had expressed interest in me, I'd rejected him, and he was afraid I was going to hit him. He was afraid he would end up like Mark and Dionte.

Smart-ass twenty-two-year-old me assumed I knew every fear a black man could possibly have walking down the street. Police harassment/violence. Fitting the description and being identified as a suspect. A nigga scuffing your kicks and a fight breaking out. Never once did I consider being assaulted for expressing your attractions.

And it's because in every definition of "man" I could conceive, the default sexual identity I envisioned was straight. A "man" was different from a "gay man," as if "gay" as an adjective modifies the noun "man" to the point of it becoming something altogether different. And if "man" was different from "gay man," then it followed naturally that "black man" was different from "black gay man," and while the issues facing black gay men were important, they were separate from those of black men. Separate, and not at all equal.

They weren't equal because not only have we turned black gay men into punch lines, we have established them as the ultimate bogeyman. Author J. L. King caused mass hysteria by "uncovering" the "down low" in his bestselling book *On the Down Low*. In the mid-aughts, you'd have believed the "down low" was an actual place, a morally bankrupt dungeon housed ten stories below every major urban center with a large black population. It was meant to describe black men having sex with other men and not telling their wives and girlfriends. Cheating, in a nutshell. But the fact they were cheating with other men was cause for full-blown crisis language. Suddenly we were in the midst of an epidemic being diagnosed by TV pundits, barbershop philosophers, preachers, and first-year college students alike.

As if it were a new phenomenon. Far from it, but we did now have a new name for it. As if bisexual isn't its own sexual identity. It is, but we only really consider sexuality as a binary. As if the larger deceit was the gender of the person with whom they cheated, as opposed to the deceit of cheating itself. It's not, but homophobia manifests in multiple ways. As if the greater concern was that of black women's health, because HIV/AIDS is so prevalent among gay men who could then transfer the disease to their women partners. Maybe, but when have we ever prioritized the health of black women?

And lost in the gay panic of all of this "down-low" madness were two crucial questions: 1) If the spread of HIV/AIDS was everyone's top concern, why not focus on the factors that have made it so prevalent and deadly among gay men? and 2) If everyone was so offended by these men keeping their sexual identities secret, what were any of us doing to ensure it was safe for them to "come out"?

There, again, is that awkward phrase, "come out." A society promotes a uniform identity for every person, pushes those who don't conform to that identity to the margins, then asks for a declaration of their otherness. As reward, those who "come out" are called brave, positioning everyone who hasn't as a coward, and yet they are still denied their full rights, their newfound bravery their only comfort.

To the extent that we still need a term for declaring your marginalized sexual (or gender) identity to the world, I've opted to go with one I learned from my friend Darnell L. Moore—"inviting in." It's a meaningful shift in language that no longer places the burden of bravery on the marginalized to "come out" to a hostile world. "Inviting in" recognizes that it isn't the marginalized who should be responsible for the terms of their own identity, but those who have made that identity dangerous to embrace.

But as necessary as that shift is, what we still have now is people "coming out" to a hostile world. And so long as the world remains hostile, some people will retreat to the relative safety of the "down-low" dungeons.

I use "people" here, but the "down low" is something attributed specifically to black men, as though black men are more prone to sexual deception than any others. It feeds another narrative—that it's more difficult to "come out" as a black gay man because black communities are aggressively more homophobic than anyone else.

To pretend black people aren't homophobic would be disingenuous, but to pretend like homophobia is some peculiarly black problem is part of a racist pathologizing that turns black people and cultures into the scapegoats for all of America's social ills. Black people have formed unique cultures out of our experiences here, but we are, if nothing else, American. The best and worst of America is reflected in us, and homophobia is no exception. We did not declare homosexuality a mental illness, nor did we write the laws forbidding sodomy or legalize firing a person for their sexual identity. We have absorbed this culture of bigotry through the same institutions as everyone else.

But the way the myth persists, you would think it's black people who run into the homes of white gay youth and reject them into homelessness and poverty, and that it's black people's backwardness that prolonged the fight for marriage equality. That narrative gained steam after the 2008 election. In 2004, it was widely believed that George W. Bush was able to capture as large a percentage of the black vote as he did by making same-sex marriage discrimination a key part of his platform, and then appealing to black religious leaders who preached homosexuality as a sin. In 2008, California's Proposition 8, a ballot initiative aimed at taking away same-sex marriage rights, passed due to an increased turnout of black voters showing up to elect Barack Obama, so the thinking went. It's true that a majority of black voters did vote in favor of stripping same-sex marriage rights, but it was more like 58 percent, far less than the 70 percent that exit polls suggested. And at only 10 percent of the overall vote they weren't enough to determine Prop 8's fate. Further, it was more a generational split than anything, with older voters strongly supporting Prop 8, while younger/first-time voters of all races were more likely to vote to uphold same-sex marriage's legality.

But the narrative became so entrenched in American punditry that when President Obama finally evolved on the issue of same-sex marriage and became the first sitting U.S. president to endorse it, there was concern that he would either depress black voter turnout or lose a significant percentage in the 2012 election. The result was that for the first time in history a larger percentage of eligible black voters showed up to the polls than whites, and 93 percent of them voted to reelect Obama—a decrease of three percentage points from the 2008 election.

Still, black people are less likely to support marriage equality than white people, even now that it is the law of the land. But white evangelicals are the group least likely to support same-sex marriage. It is those who are unaffiliated with any religion who show the most support, suggesting that it's religion, as opposed to race, that is a bigger factor in a person's attitude toward marriage equality. On the whole, black people are more religious (Christian, specifically) than white people, so it would follow that a higher percentage of black people oppose same-sex marriage.

But this is an imperfect barometer for measuring homophobia, the same as feelings about interracial marriage are insufficient in determining how prevalent racism continues to be. I can't say from personal experience whether there's more homophobia in black communities or not; I can only listen to the stories of black gay people. They can speak for themselves.

"I'm a 34-year-old NBA center. I'm black. And I'm gay," Jason Collins wrote in the May 6, 2013, issue of *Sports Illustrated*. John Amaechi "came out" in 2007, years after his playing career had ended, making him the first NBA player to do so. But Collins, though not signed to a team at the time of his *Sports Illustrated* essay, became the first active player to be openly gay. In the four major team sports—basketball, football, baseball, hockey—there'd only been one before him, but Glenn Burke, who played for MLB's Los Angeles Dodgers and Oakland A's, isn't well remembered because the 1970s sports media shied away from reporting that part of his identity, despite his best attempts to push them into it. Collins's announcement, and finally being on an active roster the following year when he signed with the Brooklyn Nets, was monumental in using the hypervisibility offered by the current era of media to directly challenge what people's perceptions of what a gay athlete would look and sound like, setting the stage for Michael Sam to kiss his boyfriend on national television.

There had been same-sex kisses on television before, but nothing quite like the live reaction of the first openly gay football player being drafted into the NFL then turning to his partner for affection. Football players are America's gladiators, they purposefully evoke the imagery of war and soldiers—to show strength. To show vitality. To show toughness. To show masculinity. Kissing another man conveys none of these qualities. Michael Sam's presence was a direct challenge to that idea.

But he never got a real chance to mount that challenge. For all the excitement surrounding Sam's history-making entrance into the NFL, it was very short-lived. He was seventh-round draft pick of the St. Louis Rams and failed to make the team after the preseason, then was picked up by the Dallas Cowboys practice squad from which he was also let go. After a brief stint in the Canadian Football League, where he became their first openly gay player, Sam retired, citing concerns for his mental health.

Jason Collins hadn't fared much better, though he was a veteran near the end of his career at the time of his announcement. He signed with the Nets toward the end of the 2013–14 NBA season, played twenty-two games, then retired. Whatever potential for shifting people's perceptions of gay athletes and masculinity that Collins and Sam represented was never realized because hardly anyone got to see them.

Still, their contributions can't be made into historical footnotes. However brief their visibility, they made a nation pay attention and ask itself some important questions. But the answer we seemed to have settled on is that we're not ready to have any answers about changing our assumptions about masculinity, especially with regard to male sexuality, unless an openly gay athlete is really, really good at one of the sports deemed most masculine. It's not only a matter of popularity that keeps us from caring whether or not an openly gay male (because the other side of homophobia in sports is the assumption that most women athletes are lesbians) has success in a sport such as tennis or soccer. Football, basketball, baseball, and hockey are spaces where men prove their manhood.

But there's a particular concern about acceptance of gay athletes in football and basketball—the sports where black men are the dominant presence. As if black men's devotion to hypermasculinity presents a bigger challenge to acceptance than that of the nearly all-white NHL, where fighting is an expected and accepted part of the sport. But where black men are, the fear of increased homophobia follows.

It's why we ask if hip-hop is ready for an openly gay rapper and not the rest of the music world, as if the tropes of "proper" masculinity are only perpetuated by black male rappers. Mainstream culture has a tendency, once it has declared some idea uncouth, to turn black men into the scapegoats for the idea's continued existence. When someone decided we shouldn't teach our kids materialism, suddenly it was black men's penchant for jewelry and expensive cars that was to blame for anybody wanting things. When blatantly sexist language became impolite to say in public, it was black men's insistence on calling women bitches and hoes that was to blame for everyone else repeating that language. And since the American mainstream has supposedly done so much now to accept sexual identity (so long as you identify as gay), it's black men holding back progress by not celebrating an openly gay hip-hop superstar.

This isn't an excuse for the homophobia that does exist in hip-hop culture, though. We can't use the experience of one oppression to justify our participation in another. Dismissing the critique of hip-hop's homophobia as racist becomes a convenient excuse to avoid addressing the problem.

The rise of Frank Ocean helps. He's not a rapper, but the world of contemporary R&B has been almost indistinguishable from hip-hop for so long that it's more a semantics game. And he doesn't actually identify as gay, saying "the same sentiment that I have towards genres of music, I have towards a lot of labels and boxes and shit." But the letter that appeared on his Tumblr page ahead of the release of his 2012 debut album *Channel ORANGE* was a game changer, precisely because it wasn't a "coming out." He invited us in.

"I met somebody," the singer wrote. "I was 19 years old. *He was too.* We spent that summer, and the summer after, together. Everyday almost. And on the days we were together, *time would glide.* Most of the day I'd see him, and his smile. *I'd hear his conversation and his silence . . .* until it was time to sleep. *Sleep I would often share with him. By the time I realized I was in love, it was malignant. It was hopeless. There was no escaping, no negotiating with the feeling. No choice. It was my first love, it changed my life."*

Anyone who has ever felt romantic love for another person could relate to what Frank Ocean was describing: longing for another person's touch, preferring their silence over any other sound, wondering and hoping the feelings are reciprocated. He hit on something else all too familiar: unrequited love. It's universal. But when it's a young black man associated with hip-hop speaking on his love for another man, it seems unique.

Because it's not something any of us are accustomed to. Unless you were highly knowledgeable about the subculture of gay rappers/singers, Frank Ocean's invitation to the rest of us into his same-sex attraction was not "normal." He let us see him, all of him, and it made listening to *Channel OR-ANGE* a revolutionary moment (it didn't hurt that it was critically acclaimed and a commercial success). But how many of us, accustomed to hearing our highly sexualized crooning heroes use their instruments to woo any nondescript woman within listening distance, were ready to sing along to Frank Ocean pine after a man?

As a kid, whenever I liked a song a woman was singing about a man, I'd replace all the references to "boy" with "girl," and "man" with "girl." I was afraid to sing the lyrics as written because what if someone heard me and thought I was gay? As an adult, knowing that's a ridiculous fear to have, singing along to Frank Ocean pining after a man still felt "unnatural." The fear was no longer there, but my tongue hadn't caught up with my politics. I was relating to the sentiment behind the song "Forrest Gump," but feeling my mouth fall flat trying to sing "you're on my mind, boy."

It speaks to how deeply ingrained bigotry can become and why vigilant self-reflection is needed to undo those lessons. "In black music, we've got so many leaps and bounds to make with acceptance and tolerance in regard to that issue," Frank Ocean told *GQ*. "Some of my heroes coming up talk recklessly like that." We grew up listening to artists essentially embracing what Ice Cube once said: "True niggas ain't gay." And it made sense to us.

But that didn't start with the music. So much of my early political education was guided by readings from a time and place where, with few exceptions, it went unquestioned that when you said "the black man" you meant "heterosexual." Save for James Baldwin, I didn't spend time with many black gay/queer thinkers early on, and much less with anyone actually talking about sexuality. But with Baldwin it was all *The Fire Next Time*, not *Giovanni's Room*. And even Baldwin, though, said "the black man" and meant "heterosexual," for reasons similar to why black women were not considered when saying "black people." So much of the understanding of what liberation for black people looked like was predicated on the notion of the patriarchal model of family—that when black men, unencumbered by racism, were allowed to return to their rightful place as head of a household with their wives and children, we would, as a race, truly be free.

In one way, the strong desire for this traditional family structure among black Americans makes sense. For a people who have historically had their families destroyed because they were considered property and sold away at the discretion of a slave owner, and later through state-sanctioned violence and economic depravement, the longing for the bonds of family are deep, true, and unwavering. But what we haven't done is consider that "family" does not have to look like a husband-and-wife turned father-and-mother, with a hierarchical structure that places the husband/father in the position of leadership, his word the final say in any decision making. Through circumstance, we've built family structures that look nothing like this yet still romanticize the patriarchal model, implying the deficiency of all others.

Black gay men, then, are not only seen to be rejecting the edicts of a Christian God, but also their duties to the community and our liberation. If the key to liberation is rebuilding the black family, and family is only understood through the union of a man and woman in marriage, any man unwilling to assume that role is standing in the way of our collective progress. Not only is this a myopic view of what the struggle for freedom entails, it serves to reinforce the most oppressive aspects of the patriarchal family structure, in which everyone is subservient to the male head of household. Moreover, it assumes a singular vision of masculinity—one where being gay will never fit.

There's no room for redefinition of masculinity from this view because it's one of the key traits of masculinity—strength—that will save us. We can't afford any weakness in the face of white supremacy. True niggas can't be gay because gay isn't strength.

"Most American white men are trained to be fags" is the first sentence of Amiri Baraka's (then LeRoi Jones) 1965 essay "American Sexual Reference: Black Male." "For this reason," he continues, "it is no wonder their faces are weak and blank, left with the hurt that reality makes—anytime. That red flush, those silk blue faggot eyes." It's a recurrent theme in some black nationalist circles, that homosexuality is a white "thing," that black men who identify as gay are aligning themselves with an unnatural white creation meant to undermine our collective manhood.

Black gay men—weak, deceptive, traitors, invisible. Yet they have and continue to stand up for a black liberation that has failed to imagine them. "We believe in liberation," Darnell L. Moore writes. "Black liberation is love. And love is the radical act of removing any barrier that keeps us apart. We will, in fact, never collectively get free if our politics are weakened by lovelessness."

We haven't been brave enough to love the black gay men who have invited us in. We've attempted to define them out of the movement. We greeted Mark and Dionte's deaths with silence. But we can change.

We have the capacity for self-reflection if we're willing to tap into it. President Obama evolved. Amiri Baraka did, too.

They did so through hard listening and wrestling with their own discomfort. They let go of long-held beliefs. They recognized there were real lives being damaged on the other side of their ideas. They moved into acceptance.

But true self-reflection won't only result in an acceptance that continues to separate. It will mean unpacking our identities that have been rooted in archaic notions of masculinity and sexuality, and embracing the parts of ourselves we've been taught to reject. It will allow for a broader range of intimate expression with people of different genders. It will help us see more clearly the myriad ways these definitions of manhood have stifled our growth. Then the acceptance won't just be external. Acceptance will become too weak of a word. We'll only be able to describe it as love.

Chapter 6

The summer I decided to learn everything was the first time I read bell hooks. I didn't know which books I was supposed to read, what the classic feminist texts were, just that I needed to read bell hooks in order to bolster my black intellectual credentials. I went to Barnes & Noble and grabbed the only book of hers they had in the "African-American Interests" section—*Rock My Soul: Black People and Self-Esteem*. I read it fairly quickly and decided it was one of the most important books I had read. Then I promptly forgot all about it.

It was important because it was the first place I'd encountered any kind of discussion about black people and mental health. "I have found myself saying again and again that mental health is the revolutionary antiracist frontier African Americans must collectively explore," hooks wrote. She touched on issues of self-hatred, depression, addiction, and overall emotional well-being. This was important because one of the important black thinkers was telling me it was important. Whatever was hurting black people, I wanted to know and I wanted to fight it. But the more I read that didn't mention self-hatred, depression, addiction, and overall emotional well-being, the less important it all became. With a backlog of issues ranging from the War on Drugs to racist public education, depression seemed a low priority. I knew people who were locked up; I didn't know anyone who was depressed. It was easy to forget.

I had my first panic attack when I was sixteen. George W. Bush was gearing up for war in Iraq, and all the messaging about weapons of mass destruction had its intended effect on me, knotting up fear of death and destruction in my gut. I didn't have a way of understanding what was happening, and I didn't feel comfortable talking to my parents about it. I was already afraid of anthrax and random terrorist attacks, but war was another beast. War was something we read about in history books or saw in Oscar-winning movies. Of course, the United States was already at war in Afghanistan after 9/11, but no one called it that. This was *real* war, and all the history books and movies led me to believe it was this all-consuming affair in which every person should fear for their life. I had even more reason to be scared, living near the world's largest naval station. George W. Bush was putting my young life in danger.

Not too long after the bombing campaign in Iraq began, we had a power outage. Had there been a storm that night, this wouldn't have struck me as unusual, but there was no storm. A power line had fallen somewhere nearby, and while the outage didn't last long, the momentary loss of power spooked me. I was sitting at my computer, logged into an AOL chat room, and talking about how wack mainstream rap music was, but now I was certain we were under attack.

And while I tried to go about the evening assuming everything was normal, I couldn't shake the feeling that the bombs were coming and I was going to die that night. I went to wash the dishes and saw an odd bright flash of light in the distance, and it's unfamiliarity screamed "nuclear bomb" to me. I stepped away from the window and ran up to my room and quietly freaked the fuck out.

I paced. I thought it would calm me down. I paced and shook my arms and breathed intently, long, hard breaths. Nothing was working. I saw the bombs landing, our house crumbling, our neighbors in the streets shouting in agony, the tears I'd cry knowing death was only seconds away. With each passing moment, I tried to convince myself that since none of that had come to pass, I could relax. But I was afraid that once I relaxed, that's when all hell would break loose. I didn't want to panic, but I also thought my panic was the only thing keeping me alive.

I sat back in front of my computer, went back to those chat rooms, but couldn't steel myself against my fears. Every few minutes I would jump up, pace, shake, and breathe. The house made sounds, normal settling or movement, but each time it did my fear was renewed. I ran to my parents' room on the brink of tears.

I collapsed right into my mother's arms and she asked, "What's wrong, baby? You're shaking. Calm yourself." I didn't know what to say, only that I needed her to hold me. And she did, while I mustered up the courage to say, "I'm scared." I was too embarrassed to tell her why. But she couldn't help me to not be scared if I refused to talk. My father, standing on the other side of the bed, reminded me of that.

When I'd cried enough and felt I'd calmed down enough, I went back to my room. But as soon as I did, I screamed out for help. The fear returned, the shaking. My father ran in, asking again what was wrong, and I felt even more shame. I lay down on my bed. He pulled up a chair next to me. He waited.

"I'm scared . . . the news . . . they keep talking about war . . . and Saddam Hussein . . . and all these weapons of mass destruction. . . ." That's all the incoherence I could get out. "Son, you don't need to worry," he said. "I served in the military for twenty years, do you think I spent all that time in something that's weak and couldn't handle this? You should stop watching the news for a while."

And then he left. And I was left to contemplate what he said. The military would keep me safe. America's mighty, mighty military. They wouldn't let me die. This was supposed to bring me comfort.

For a short time, it did. But that lasted all of ten minutes, right as the sounds of the outside world once again had me convinced that America's military might didn't mean shit and we were all about to die. But that's not what I talked about when I went to my parents' room this time. I told them that something had to be wrong with me, because my heart kept beating too fast and my hands kept shaking. I needed to see a doctor. I needed to see a doctor immediately.

My father drove me to the hospital. He filled out the paperwork. I sat as quietly as I could. I was trying to beat the images of my death out of my head. We sat in the waiting room for what seemed like forever, until the nurses, who had decided based on my age and relative good health that the symptoms I was experiencing couldn't be too serious, asked why I felt it was so urgent. I told them the story of what happened. Now it was being interpreted as a potential electrocution since I was at my computer when the power went out, a room would open up faster.

The doctor came in and inspected me. Pulse check, reflex check, pupil check, and all. He determined I hadn't been electrocuted. "It sounds like you just had a panic attack," he said. And then we were dismissed.

The only exposure I'd had to the phrase "panic attack" was an episode of the UPN show *Malcolm & Eddie*, where Malcolm Jamal-Warner's character was having panic attacks and couldn't figure out what was wrong with him, but once he discovered they were "just" panic attacks he was able to move on. It was "just" a panic attack I had. The doctor didn't seem worried. It was over. I was ready to move on.

I didn't think it was a symptom of anything larger, even though they kept occurring periodically. They would come without the same stimulus as the first one. I would be sitting and watching TV and suddenly feel like my heart was beating too slowly, at which point I'd get up and pace around, only this would cause my heart to beat too fast, but sitting still let it slow down too much. I'd pace, shake, and breathe through it. Their lengths varied, from five minutes to two hours. But it was "just" a panic attack, and they only happened about once a month. They didn't pose any threat to my physical health. As soon as I came down from one, I'd convinced myself there was nothing to worry about.

They were nothing to worry about all the way up, and then through, my first major depression a year later. I'm only calling it depression in hindsight. I wasn't diagnosed because it wasn't something I thought I needed to talk about, and I likely wouldn't have seen a professional even if I did. It was just a rough patch, a natural part of the human experience. You can't be winning all the time. My grades had slipped before. There was nothing to worry about. I'd been sad about an unrequited crush before. There was nothing to worry about. I was naturally quiet and withdrawn. There was nothing to worry about.

But sleeping only two or three hours a night, that was new. Not being "in the mood" to eat, even when I was hungry, that was new. Imagining people's reactions to my death, considering if everyone would be happier if I were dead, writing these thoughts down, that was new. Being angry at myself for having these thoughts in the first place, that was new.

Mrs. Copeland, my guidance counselor, was trying to help me through the rest of the school year and make sure I made it to college, but she could see that I was struggling. She tried to give me a pep talk. "You're down now, but you've got to get up and get back in the race," she said.

"I feel like I've fallen facedown on the track and I'm sinking into it. I can't see my way back up," I told her.

The only times I felt any semblance of life is when I felt the rush of stealing CDs from Best Buy, or when I was trading in the AOL chat rooms for online porn. None of this signaled depression to me. I wanted more music than I could afford, so I stole, and I was frustrated by my lack of sexual experience, so I watched porn. And what's abnormal about a seventeen-year-old committing petty theft or being horny? There was nothing to worry about.

A year later I read *Rock My Soul* and I didn't make any connection to what I had experienced. None of what hooks was talking about in terms of depression or anxiety or suicidal thoughts resonated on a personal level. I saw in her words something plaguing black communities, not myself. I was a college student. Sober. And aside from the occasional profanity-laced tirade against a U.S. Marine, emotionally stable. I was perfectly sane.

Three years later, I failed to make the connection again when I just stopped going to class. It had always been difficult for me to maintain any interest in school, but I had done enough to get by, get into college, and not totally piss off my professors because of my "wasted potential." But I was finding it harder to pretend. I entered my senior year needing about eighteen credit hours to graduate, which, split up over two semesters, meant a very light course load. The only thing that required any real attention was my senior thesis.

After "Hampton University hates black people," though, I ignored everything to wholly commit to my work at the newspaper and my growing campus activism. I half-assed the first part of my thesis, earning a C– when I needed at least a C in order to move on to the second part. That minus seemed spiteful. But with a second semester loaded with electives and an 8 a.m. tennis class, the thesis could have all of the attention I didn't give to the newspaper. Everything else just required me to show up.

At some point, I stopped showing up. Eight a.m. tennis was the first casualty, because the entire concept of that class at that time should be outlawed. I wanted to sleep. And the later I slept, the more classes I sacrificed. I chalked it up to senioritis. For a stretch of two or three weeks, I gave a valiant effort, even showing up to class on time. But after midterms, I was practically a ghost.

I didn't even bother with the thesis. Every day, I would tell myself that I was going to go to the library tomorrow and really get into the research. And when tomorrow came, I would tell myself it would be better if I waited until next week, when I would really be able to focus. My thesis adviser never saw me.

I kept making it to the newspaper office. It was the only thing that could convince me to get out of bed on the days where I wanted to sleep until 4, 5, and 6 p.m, which was happening more often. But even on those days, I managed to talk myself into rolling out of bed, throwing on a pair of unwashed jeans and a wrinkled polo, and driving to campus so I could guide my team while we produced an award-winning newspaper.

More often than not, my only meal of the day came during those late nights in the newspaper office. A postmidnight run to McDonald's, the only restaurant in the area serving late night, aside from IHOP. Some fries and dollar menu sweet tea was my entire diet.

On the rare day when I did go to class and there was no pressing newspaper business to attend to, I would go home and open up the bottle of cheap vodka that I had taken to keeping around. I didn't drink, in earnest, until I was twenty-one. Not because I was a stickler for legality, but I was scared that being drunk would be some type of out of body experience, where I would somehow be outside of myself watching my body do things that I had no control over. By the beginning of 2008, I'd abandoned that fear and drank that ice-cold vodka more days than not.

Everyday I was lying to people. "How are you?" they would ask. "I'm fine," I would say. That was enough to satisfy most people because they weren't actually asking, only exchanging pleasantries. The few that genuinely wanted to know would follow up, "Are you sure?"

I would smile and lie again. "Yeah, of course. Why wouldn't I be?"

The more I lied, the more I wanted to believe the lie, the less I could. Every time I said I was fine, I saw myself dying. Sometimes I saw myself slitting my wrists. Sometimes I saw myself intentionally crashing my car. Sometimes I saw myself buying a gun and shooting myself through the mouth and the back of my head. Sometimes I saw myself jumping from a tall building, felt the wind beneath me, frightened and free.

Visions of my own death had kept me up nights since I was three years old, terrifying me. This was the first time I'd imagined what it would look and feel like to kill myself. It was my fear of death that prevented me from acting on any of those thoughts, but it wasn't strong enough to keep me from having them, from considering the possibility. And no matter how frequent these thoughts were, I didn't stop lying. I couldn't. It would pass, I told myself. It was just the stress of managing the newspaper while trying to graduate and figure out what I was going to do with my postcollege life getting to me. I could shake it off. There was nothing to worry about.

"Have you lost weight? You're looking skinny. I mean, you're skinny, but you look thinner," my economics professor said to me. Without notice, my size 30 waist jeans that used to fit comfortably on my hips now required me to pull my belt a couple notches tighter to keep from sagging. I hadn't given it a thought until she said something. "I haven't seen you much, I figured you were pledging." I laughed. I went home and looked in the mirror. I worried for the first time that something was really wrong. I cried.

I reached a point where I wanted to talk, but I didn't know about what or with whom. Leslie and I had broken up. More accurately, she broke up with me because I pushed her away. Right around the time I realized I was in love with her, I passive-aggressively asked if we could take a break and see other people, then changed my mind, then continued to withdraw emotionally until she ended things. We were attempting a friendship, but in order to draw the lines, she wasn't as available to me. I still wouldn't have known what to say.

I stopped answering my mother's phone calls. She was the only other person I would have talked to and I was pushing her away, as well. I pushed away the people it was hard to lie to.

The vodka in my freezer stopped being helpful. I didn't stop drinking it, but it no longer soothed me. I didn't want to drink anymore; I had to.

I had never smoked weed before, for reasons similar to why it took me so long to drink. But I grew more and more curious, the more people I had around me who did smoke and the less comfort drinking brought me. I decided I would try it, so a friend came over and showed me how to smoke a bowl. I had no idea what I was doing and was sure I didn't do it right because I didn't feel anything afterward. I drove her back to her dorm room, and on my way home it hit me. It wasn't bad.

A couple weeks later, she came back with three more people and we rolled a blunt in my car. I was getting turned off by all the spit required to make this happen, and how the loose, wet blunt felt in my mouth when it came around to me. Regardless, I inhaled the smoke, trying to make sure I felt it immediately this time.

Something was off in the middle of my chest. The blunt was done and again I wasn't sure if I was high. I didn't feel how everyone else looked. Something in my chest was tight. I burped. Just gas, I thought. There was nothing to worry about.

I got out of the car, waved good-bye to my fellow smokers and walked back to my apartment. The tightness in my chest returned. It's just gas, I thought. Just get it out. There's nothing to worry about.

It wasn't coming out this time. There was tingling in my left arm. I couldn't breathe normally, every breath needed to be deep, long, powerful. I couldn't get enough air. I walked into my apartment as calmly as possible. Justin and Brandon were home. "Hey Mychal," Justin said. I couldn't get enough air. My left arm went numb. I went to feel my heartbeat, but I didn't need to. I saw it pounding outside of my chest.

"Justin . . . take me to the hospital."

He didn't hesitate to pick up his car keys and rush me to the car. I sat on the passenger side, screaming, "I think I'm having a heart attack!" I rolled down the window. I stuck my head out like a dog wanting to wag its tongue. I couldn't get enough air. I knew we weren't going to make it. I knew I was dying. I cried.

"Just breathe, we almost there," Justin tried to reassure me. "I can't. I can't breathe. I feel like I'm having a heart attack," I told him, having never had a heart attack and not knowing what one would feel like. The adrenaline had me convinced that I was moving faster than everything around me, including the car. I felt like it was taking forever to get to the hospital, which may have been for the best. Real or imagined, the long ride to the hospital gave me a chance to gather myself, to find my breath. When we finally arrived, I was breathing much better and my heart was back in my chest. Walking toward the doors, I collapsed into tears. Justin and Brandon held me. I told them I wanted to go home.

But as I sobbed through the ride home, the tingling in my left arm returned. My heart started beating too fast again. I couldn't get enough air. "Take me back to the hospital," I told Justin. He didn't ask questions. He made the U-turn and got me back to the hospital.

Justin filled out the paperwork while I stared at the waiting room walls. I was coming down and feeling closer to normal, but thought I should get checked out just in case something was actually wrong. "I'm sorry," I said to Justin, but he dismissed my apology and sat by my side until I was called back to be seen by a doctor. The nurses performed their duties, taking my blood pressure and temperature, then left me on my own to wait. I lay in a ball on the hospital bed, reflecting on each moment of the night that led me there. I wasn't crying anymore, but I could barely speak above a strained whisper when the doctor finally came in. He checked my heart rate, the dilation of my pupils, my reflexes. "Have you done anything abnormal tonight?" he asked. "I smoked weed for the first time," I admitted. "Welp, I guess you learned your lesson, right?"

"Yeah," I managed. He left. I got back into the ball. The nurses dismissed me. Justin drove me home. I crawled into bed and slept.

It was the first time since I was sixteen that a panic attack had landed me in the hospital. But since it was helped along by the weed, I wrote it off as an anomaly that only revealed that weed wasn't meant to be one of my vices. I even told people the story. "How are you?" they'd ask. "I had a massive panic attack that put me in the hospital," I'd say. "Oh my god, are you okay?" they'd ask. "Yeah, I'm fine, just probably never going to smoke weed again. Haha, not my drug of choice. There's nothing to worry about."

But by the end of March, it was getting harder to make the lie believable. With increasing frequency, my parents asked if I was sure I was going to graduate on time. I hadn't picked up graduate invites. I hadn't purchased a cap and gown. I hadn't set an appointment for an exit interview. I still wasn't going to class. I hadn't even pretended to try to revise my thesis. "Yeah, I should," I told them. "I'll have to do a summer course to finish my thesis, but I'll be able to walk."

To tell the truth would have been to admit failure. I didn't want to fail and face my mother's disappointment and my father's lecture. I was not only their firstborn but part of the first generation in both of their families to send several children to college. My graduating was a sign of progress, a sign of a job well done. I wasn't even making it out of my bed most days.

I went home one weekend and found my mother in the backyard getting her plants ready for summer. She asked me, "So, how are we doing this, when school is over, are you coming back here? What room are you taking?" I started crying.

"What's wrong, my child?"

"I don't know. Everything."

Her hands were covered in soil and she didn't want to get me dirty by holding me, so she called my father over. He embraced me and walked me back into the house. I sat on the couch and cried until I physically couldn't any longer.

I told my parents what I felt. Some of it. I told them I wasn't sleeping, that I hadn't been going to class, that there was basically no way I was going to graduate on time, that I had been feeling pressure, that I didn't know what I wanted to do with my life, that I was feeling like a failure, that I was afraid of disappointing them and everyone else. My father said, "It sounds like you're going through some sort of depression."

There was the word. It was finally out there. I was relieved to hear it because what I was feeling had a name that I could say. But it was an empty consolation, because a name is just a name. I still didn't know what to do about it. I didn't know how to get better.

At present, I can say I've known many people who lived with depression, but that's a retroactive designation based on what I know about the illness and people's behavior. No one in my life when I was twenty-one years old would have said they had depression. Plenty of people said they were "depressed," which generally meant "really sad," but no one would cop to the mental illness and its attending characteristics. I thought no one I knew would have gotten close enough to a psychiatrist to be diagnosed. The only people I "knew" who had gone to a psychiatrist and would talk about it openly were white people in Woody Allen movies.

White people in the professional and artistic classes have been able to wear their weekly analyst sessions as a badge of intellect for some time now, while the rest of us labor under the stigma of mental illness and mental health care, a stigma especially strong in black communities. Of course, black people have every reason to be distrustful of mental health care in this country; mental institutions have largely functioned as another form of prison, and black people have been assigned mental illnesses to completely rational behaviors. But that doesn't mean we don't suffer, often in silence.

Black people pride ourselves on the fact that we have survived in America despite having every form of violence inflicted upon us. We've made it through slavery and lynchings, rape and Jim Crow, poverty and police dogs, fire hoses and jail cells, and on the other side have raised families and created culture that's emulated (and stolen) the world over. With every odd imaginable set against us, we have persevered through the strength of our collective will and faith in

Jesus. But neither our will, nor faith, can adequately heal the psychic wounds of that survival.

While black women are burdened with strength and silence in order to shoulder the emotional needs of the entire community, men tend to inherit a sense of masculinity that teaches stoicism as a virtue. There are generations of black boys and men walking around with turmoil swelling inside of them ready to explode at any minute. I learned very early on to suppress my emotions. "The violence done to black boys is the abusive insistence, imposed on them by family and by society, that they not feel," bell hooks wrote in the book I thought was massively important and promptly forgot. I was a sensitive child; the slightest bit of teasing from my big cousins, whose approval I desperately wanted, would set me off into tears. But that only made it harder to endear myself to them, because now they couldn't hang out with me without me "crying like a little girl." My other options were to strike back verbally, which I was never quick or brave enough for, or give into the urge to fight them, which may have earned their respect but also would have meant an ass-whooping. I tried to laugh along or be silent.

And when I wasn't being directly instructed to shut off my emotions, I learned by example. My father was a picture-perfect example of masculine authority. My brother and I knew him as provider and strict disciplinarian. That's all. I can only guess now at what made him afraid, what caused him pain, what trauma he lived through to become the man he did. Those weren't stories he shared, emotions he was willing to offer. He always said we could talk to him about anything, but he never opened up, and I learned to never open up, either.

I always waited until it was too late. I waited until the rage, or pain, or sadness was unbearable, when it left me facedown on the track and sinking. Then things would come pouring out of me, and I'd feel much better, but never carry the lesson forward. I wanted to change that, but I didn't know how.

As much as I wanted to change, my family wanted to help. Aunt Gay, my mother's twin who cared for me like she had birthed me herself, called me the next day and reassured me she was proud and that I would be alright. Not too long after, Darius, one of Aunt Gay's sons, called and told me that I had nothing to be ashamed of, that I had accomplished more than so many young black men get the chance to, that I should be proud. I appreciated the pep talks, and told them as much, but they weren't what I needed. I told Aunt Gay to tell Antaeus, her oldest son, to call me. He was the only person I knew who would relate.

"How do you do it?" I asked him almost as soon as I picked up the phone. Confused, Antaeus asked, "How do I do what?"

Crying, I answered, "How do you live without Demetri?"

Demetri was born on February 27, 1982, the first of Roberta and Clayton Sr.'s grandchildren to be born in the 1980s. He was the firstborn son of my mother's only brother, Clayton Jr. I always looked up to him because Demetri didn't tease as hard as everyone else. I felt protected around him. He was the best at everything: basketball, football, every video game. I would practice Mortal Kombat and Street Fighter at home with the explicit goal of trying to get good enough to beat Demetri on our next trip to D.C. I saw Antaeus, Darius, and Marcus, Aunt Gay's sons, more often, but Demetri held a special place. He was my big cousin. I looked up to him.

My mother disappeared for a few days in March 1999. On a rare occasion, she would go see her family without us, so it didn't strike me as abnormal. Then my father called for my brother and I to come downstairs. Demetri had been shot, he said. Seven times, he said. Your mother is in D.C. now, he said. I didn't grasp the gravity of the situation because he never said, "Demetri is dead." Instead, he turned the moment into a lecture about why he was always telling us that "choices" were important, and we should always make the right choices. Demetri had sold drugs before, though he wasn't at the time of the shooting. My big cousin was dead and my father was admonishing me about "choices."

I didn't know Demetri was dead until the three of us arrived in D.C., the day before the funeral. I had to piece it together on my own. Up to that point, I thought we were just going to visit him in the hospital. I walked into the church and immediately started crying. I didn't want to see the body. I was taken out of the viewing line and a number of people attempted to console me, but who could? We had been to a number of funerals in my short twelve years, but none with circumstances this tragic. I finally made it up to the casket, where Demetri lay lifeless, his Afro as neat as could be, but my body felt out of place and time. I wanted to be anywhere else.

I took a seat in a pew, my little brother next to me, and all that went through my head was "Demetri is dead. Demetri is dead. Demetri is dead." I saw Andre, Demetri's younger brother, walk up to the casket. The whispers started. Many people thought it was Andre's fault Demetri was shot. Demetri wasn't supposed to be there. Andre asked him to be there. The exact details and circumstances never really interested me. My big cousin was dead and it didn't matter to me how it happened.

At the cemetery, I walked up to Uncle Clayton and held him for far too long. He was holding it together as best he could. He shouldn't have had to bury his son. Having already lost the love of his life, Demetri's mother, and now Demetri, everyone worried about him. He was HIV positive, and it was never really clear how much longer he would be with us. None of these things crossed my mind. I just needed to hug my uncle and cry. So I did.

At Aunt Connie's house, there was food. I barely touched anything, save for the half a chicken breast and some collard greens my mother made sure I ate. I couldn't look at anyone. Everything felt wrong.

Uncle Clayton had a little to drink, as he was wont to do. He was trying to forget, or at least take the edge off. "You still got that jump shot?" he asked me, while I could smell the alcohol on his breath. I tried a smile for him. Last time he visited us in Virginia Beach we had played basketball in the driveway together and he was impressed by my jump shot. I was proud of that. "Next time I come down, I wanna see it, you hear me?" He was trying to make me feel better. For him, I kept the tears from coming down. I struggled through a half-hearted laugh, nodded my head, and said, "Yeah. Okay."

We never got that chance. Uncle Clayton died the next year.

I mentioned to my parents that Demetri's death impacted me during my first major depression. They had a talk with me after discovering I used my credit card to pay for online porn. Halfway through, I broke down crying. They were saying they weren't mad, but I wasn't crying about that. "What is it?" they asked. "Something that happened a long time I ago," I replied.

"To you?"

"No."

"To your mother? To your brother? To your Aunt Gay?"

"My cousin."

"He's talking about Demetri," my mother said, before rushing to my side to hug me while I cried uncontrollably. Demetri had been dead for five years at that point, and while I thought about him every single day, I never spoke about what I felt. I didn't know who I could talk to. No one ever spoke about Demetri. My mother didn't. She had lost a nephew to gun violence and never mentioned it. We were a "laugh to keep from crying" kind of family. It's not an ideal way to reach out in a time of need. Laughing to keep from crying only helps when everyone knows what you're laughing about.

I thought I had moved on. I thought I had Demetri in my heart and memories and that's all I needed. But four years later I acknowledged the pain, I asked Antaeus, the only person I knew who had been as deeply affected by Demetri's death as I was, how he made it through each day without him.

We talked for probably an hour. Antaeus told me how hard it was for him, why he had gotten his tattoos, one of Demetri's nickname on his forearm, why we had to keep going despite it all. It helped, a little. It helped to know I wasn't alone with my pain.

I heard from Aunt Connie next. She started with a similar pep talk like the ones I had gotten from Aunt Gay and Darius, but then I started talking about Demetri and things changed. "You like to write, don't you?" she said to me. "Then you use those words. You use those words to make sure what happened to Demetri don't have to happen to any other black boys."

Here's how I know the racists, pundits, racist pundits, and the few well-meaning folks who say "What about black-on-black violence?" as a means of diverting attention away from conversations about police violence and white supremacy aren't sincere: they never express any concern about the trauma experienced by those left behind. In the rush to lock everyone away, the political class never stops to ask what kind of mental health care a community that deals with violence daily may need. Black people of all ages and genders are walking around with post-traumatic stress disorder, depression, anxiety, and survivor's guilt without anywhere to turn. We attempt to heal our broken insides with whatever is available. More often that not, what's available are the most unhealthy options. We overdose on liquor and drugs, unprotected sex, violence, and repression because that's all there is to help us cope. It's important not to pathologize this kind of behavior as uniquely black, because everyone self-medicating an undiagnosed mental illness is susceptible, but at the same time we have to recognize that this is all that's offered to black people in terms of help. So like every other social ill, our post-traumatic stress disorder, depression, anxiety, and survivor's guilt takes a more dangerous turn when filtered through American racism.

I didn't know to name what I was experiencing as "survivor's guilt" until months after the conversation with Aunt Connie, when I finally did get into therapy. It wasn't an easy road there. The panic attacks didn't let up, coming every day with varying degrees of intensity. I couldn't go to the bathroom without believing that I might die on the toilet. I was afraid of the clouds, because on days where they blocked the sun, I believed the darkness of death was creeping in and my time was coming. I called the hospital to tell them I was suicidal; they said I needed to make an appointment with a psychiatrist. I knew it was true, but seeing a psychiatrist would mean that I was crazy. Crazy was for white people in Woody Allen movies.

But there was nowhere else for me to go. I had two full physicals that showed whatever ailments I was convinced I had during my panic attacks weren't real. The problem had to be my brain.

Once a week, I talked to my therapist about not graduating, about Demetri, about my fear of death. She diagnosed me, officially, with depression, anxiety disorder, mild hypochondria, and introduced me to the term "survivor's guilt." It was eye-opening.

I was lucky. My family had the means and access to be able to provide me with good mental health care. In a country where public funding for mental health care is constantly being slashed, this is increasingly not true for everyone. But with so much stigma surrounding mental illness and mental health care, this hasn't become a staple of our advocacy. And even where there's acknowledgment that mental illness is real, it takes a backseat to issues like police violence, poverty, and incarceration. We fail to make the connection between these things and the prevalence of mental illnesses within our community. How many of us are watching the latest video of police assaulting or killing a young black person and slipping into depression? How many of us are being sent to prison, locked away in solitary confinement, and coming out on the other side suicidal? How many of us experience anxiety and paranoia from the stress of poverty, and lack of food, and exposure to the daily violence that becomes an outgrowth of our attempts to survive? The everyday condition of blackness in America is enough to drive you crazy, but without those connections, we've been lacking in advocates.

The first mental health advocate I met was Bassey Ikpi. We followed each other on Twitter, where her rapid-fire and hilarious tweets about pop culture were always filling up my timeline. I was impressed that she had been on Def Poetry Jam, hosted by the Mighty Mos Def, and was a favorite of every would-be black intellectual during the early to mid-2000s. More importantly, Bassey told her story of being diagnosed with bipolar II disorder. She talked openly about what it did to her mind and body, about medication and treatment facilities. We became friends in part because her bravery in laying herself bare for the world was so inspiring to me. She taught me not to be ashamed, she gave me the language of "living with" instead of "suffering from" and "I have" versus "I am." She showed me what it was to have to commit every day to getting better, and that there isn't some straight line that leads to "recovery." Bassey encouraged me to tell my story, to be to someone else what she was for me. Without her, I would still be saying there's nothing to worry about.

Without Bassey, I would have called Ron Artest crazy, too.

In his early days with the Chicago Bulls, Ron Artest would drink Hennessy during the halftime of games. As a member of the Indiana Pacers, Artest was responsible for the "Malice at the Palace," the most infamous on-court fight in NBA history, which involved several members of both the Pacers and the at-home Detroit Pistons, as well as fans, one of which had thrown a cup at Artest while he was lying on the scorer's table. He received the longest suspension for an on-court incident in NBA history. In March 2007, Artest was arrested on domestic violence charges, for which he was sentenced to twenty days in jail, ten of which he actually served. His tough defensive style on the court earned him the honor of NBA Defensive Player of the Year in 2004, but also constantly resulted in flagrant fouls, and his penchant for speaking his mind earned him a number of technicals. His postgame interviews were often referred to as "bizarre."

Ron Artest was crazy, according to any number of NBA fans. That the Los Angeles Lakers would take him on for the 2009–10 season, after they had won the championship the year before, seemed a risky move. Artest was widely regarded as one of the most talented players in the NBA, but his on- and off-court violence made him a liability.

The season went by without much incident, and the Lakers made it back to the NBA finals, where they defeated the Boston Celtics in seven games. It was the first finals appearance of Artest's career and he played a big role in helping the Lakers win the best-of-seven series. ESPN's Doris Burke got an interview with a celebratory Artest as the confetti rained down, and he ignored her first question. He needed to get out his thank yous.

"First off, I wanna thank everybody in my hood. . . ." Crazy Ron Artest was here, breaking with any sort of decorum. He thanked his wife, kids, and family. And he kept going.

"I definitely want to thank my doctor, Dr. Santhi, my psychiatrist. . . ."

I let out a very audible "oh shit" when he said that. "She really helped me relax a lot. Thank you so much. It's so difficult to play, so much emotion going on in the playoffs, and she helped me relax. I knocked down that three, just like you told me."

This was one of the greatest sports moments of my lifetime. It was so meaningful to me that it became the subject of my first professional piece of writing. Ron Artest had opened a door.

On national television, with millions watching, a six-foot-seven-inch, two-hundred-forty-pound black man from Queens, New York, who was the principal actor in the most violent spectacle ever seen on an NBA court, told us he was seeing a psychiatrist. He told us he wanted to be, and was working toward getting, better. He told us he didn't want to be broken anymore. The moment was ripe with so much potential to break down so many stigmas. But he was still, for many, just Crazy Ron Artest.

I think about people's reaction to Artest in that moment and the relative silence from black men about our mental and emotional health. Sometimes it feels like the problem is that we have internalized the perception of ourselves as unfeeling brutes. Sometimes it feels like the problem is a commitment to an antiquated idea of strength. But when we do speak, who listens? Or more critically, when we speak, what do people hear?

Hip-hop is the biggest cultural phenomenon of the past half century, taking mostly young black male voices to every place on Earth. Rappers get criticized for their materialism, sexism, homophobia, and glorification of gangster lifestyles. Whatever merit those criticisms have, and there is plenty, we're all guilty of reducing our image of rappers into caricatures, their voices into distorted versions of what we find most entertaining about black men. When they tell us what's wrong, do we listen? What do we hear?

When The Notorious B.I.G. was a "nigga rapping blunts and broads, ménage à trois, sex in expensive cars," we listened. When he was telling us his "Suicidal Thoughts," we brushed it aside. We turned "Cash Rules Everything Around Me" into a money-making anthem, without taking note of Inspectah Deck telling us, "*Though I don't know why I chose to smoke sess, I guess that's the time when I'm not depressed*, but I'm still depressed and I ask what's it worth?" When Tupac was hollering "Thug Life," everyone from vice presidential candidates to my parents wished him censored, but they couldn't be found when he was saying, "I smoke a blunt to take the pain out, and if I wasn't high I'd probably try to blow my brains out." Jay Z and Kanye West's collaborative album, *Watch the Throne*, was dismissed by some critics as "luxury rap," but what's luxurious about Jay Z saying, "Where the fuck is the prez? Where the fuck is the press? Either they don't know or don't care, I'm fucking depressed"?

When T.I. kept getting arrested on gun and drug charges, ending up in a carousel of freedom and prison, where was anyone to ask whether his behavior was a result of having witnessed so many people in his life die or go to prison, while his talents made him a millionaire celebrity, and the survivor's guilt was eating away at him?

What would happen if we reframed the way we understand black male life in a way that took mental health seriously? If we looked outside and didn't see ruthless gangbangers but teenage boys left hopeless and giving themselves suicide missions. If instead of chastising young men for fighting over sneakers we asked why they feel worthless and unseen without them. If we didn't label them junkies but rather recognized their need for affirmation. If we held our boys close when they cried instead of turning them away to face the frustration, pain, and sadness "like a man." If we believed black boys were worthy of second chances that didn't involve prison cells. What if?

We might start to worry. Then we might start to heal.

Chapter 7

At 5 a.m. on November 4, 2008, I discovered that trying to stand up after getting only one hour of sleep feels exactly like trying to stand up while drunk. The cold, wind, and annoyingly noncommittal light rain only added to the misery. For years, I remembered walking to the church, but that's a false memory my sleep-deprived mind created to enhance the tale. What actually happened is that around 4 a.m., my father knocked on my bedroom door, walked in, told me it was time to get up because the lines would be too long later in the day, and about fifteen minutes later we made the short drive to the church that served as our polling station. It was time to vote. It was time to make history.

I had decided I would vote for Barack Obama. First, I had to decide I would vote at all. Some of the guilt-tripping got to me and I feared some kind of spiritual retribution from the ancestors who had died fighting for voting rights. But there was also the pull of history. The official line is that black people didn't vote for Obama just because he's black, but aside from the terror I felt at the remote possibility of a President Sarah Palin, Obama's blackness was the major reason I had to vote for him. I was still as skeptical about electoral politics and politicians as I was at seventeen. Ideologically, Obama fell into that class of moderate Democrats that may as well have been Republicans to me. But here was the first viable black candidate for the highest office in the country, and that meant something. What, exactly, I couldn't say, or wasn't totally sure, but it was a historic moment I didn't want to look back on and not have been part of.

I was not, however, so excited about casting my first vote for the potential first black president that I felt the need to wake up at 4 a.m. and stand in line before the polls opened at 7. My father, on the other hand, couldn't wait. For the first time, he was fully behind a candidate. He donated to the campaign, put up an Obama yard sign, got a bumper sticker for his truck, added a few presidential magnets to the refrigerator door, and tuned in for every televised speech he could. And on November 4, he saw an opportunity to stand in line with his firstborn son, who would be casting his first-ever vote, and elect the country's first black president, so that's what we did. It was the kind of image that, if he had seen it, would have made Obama proud.

On the campaign trail, candidate Obama made headlines with a speech he delivered on Father's Day 2008 at Apostolic Church of God, a church on the south side of Chicago. This was his first address to a majority black audience since Hillary Clinton conceded the primary contest a week earlier and Obama became the presumptive Democratic nominee for president. That he was going to talk about fatherhood came as no shock, as it was Father's Day. That the first viable black candidate for president of the United States would use his platform to chastise black fathers was a different matter.

He began the speech with praise for Apostolic, segued into the importance of family, and ultimately spoke of how fathers are integral to the foundation of families. "But if we are honest with ourselves," he said, "we'll admit that what too many fathers also are is missing—missing from too many lives and too many homes. They have abandoned their responsibilities, acting like boys instead of men. And the foundations of our families are weaker because of it," Obama told the congregation.

"You and I know how true this is in the African-American community," he continued. "We know that more than half of all black children live in single-parent households, a number that has doubled—doubled—since we were children. We know the statistics—that children who grow up without a father are five times more likely to live in poverty and commit crime; nine times more likely to drop out of schools and twenty times more likely to end up in prison. They are more likely to have behavioral problems, or run away from home or become teenage parents themselves. And the foundations of our community are weaker because of it."

Ever since Daniel Patrick Moynihan's 1965 report "The Negro Family: The Case for National Action," which argued that the number of women-led households in black communities would be the largest obstacle to black people achieving economic and political equality, the issue of "missing black fathers" has been a top priority for black intellectuals, activists, and community leaders, as well as a favored retort from people seeking to deflect from conversations about structural racism. The thinking goes, as Obama laid out in his speech, that the high rates of poverty and incarceration, as well as the low levels of educational achievement, in black communities can be traced back to the high number of black babies born out of wedlock and subsequently raised in single-mother homes.

It's a patriarchal twist on the mythological magical negro. By their mere presence, black fathers could stem the devastating effects of oppression imposed from the classroom to the workplace to the court system. If black men just showed up in the homes of their children—acted like men instead of boys—black families and communities would fortify themselves and our long-held problems would simply wither away.

It's hard to know where to begin in untangling the many well-meaning but wrongheaded ideas wrapped inside the "missing black fathers" ideology. For starters, the statistics around black babies born out of wedlock and living in single-mother-led households don't actually tell us about the engagement of fathers. Being born to an unwed couple doesn't mean that you never have a relationship with your father. The numbers don't take into account the couples who have children and then get married later, or women who have children with one man and later partner with someone else who serves as a parent. They don't consider the number of women who choose to parent alone. They don't consider same-gender couples who, until recently, were legally barred from marriage but had chosen to parent. Without statistics that include these factors, it's impossible to know how many black children grow up without a father.

But even before unpacking the myths of black fathers' lack of involvement in their children's lives, there's the challenge of romanticizing the family structure that places a primacy on the existence and presence of men as fathers. Black nuclear families have been torn apart since the days of slavery, and since then we have also reimagined the family structure. Where the biological father and/or mother haven't been available, aunts and uncles, grandmothers and grandfathers, and a host of family friends and play cousins have stepped in to do the work of raising children. And today, as prison removes more and more black men from their homes, we continue to do the same reinvention. To say that these other family formations are inherently deficient because there isn't a father who sits atop a hierarchy of familial relationships is to say no one else is capable of providing adequate love to a child, while also teaching the children who grow up without that idealized nuclear-family model that their lives are somehow wrong. Raised to believe that they missed something vital, no matter how much love was present in their lives, it's not a surprise if children without fathers in their homes have more behavioral problems.

And that families with women-led households are more likely to live in poverty speaks less to the necessity of fathers and more to the fact that a single income is no longer sufficient to support a family in this country, that our economy undervalues the work of women, and that outside child care is a prohibitively expensive luxury. An economic shift to real living wages for women's labor and a total societal investment in the well-being of all children would solve a number of the problems we think are only alleviated by fathers.

What that would require, though, is letting go of the myth. It's hard because the "missing black father" has caused so much pain. That hurt runs through the rhetoric of every well-meaning person who has ever admonished black fathers for not being in their children's lives. It's the foundation of Barack Obama's first book and the speech he delivered before the congregation at Apostolic. That pain is real and can't be discounted, but so long as it is the only way through which we see this issue, the myth will continue to entangle us and prevent us from reckoning with what's real. The damage isn't done by the absence of a father, but from the feelings of abandonment.

If black children were raised in an environment that focused not on their lack of fathers but on filling their lives with the nurturing love we all need to thrive, what difference would an absent father make? If they woke up in homes with electricity and running water and food, went to schools with teachers and counselors who provided everything they needed to learn, then went home to caretakers of any gender who weren't so exhausted from work that they actually had time to sit and talk and do homework with them, and no one ever said that their lives were somehow incomplete because they didn't have a father, would they hold on to some pain of lack well into adulthood? This isn't an argument in favor of deadbeat fathers, but a call to detach ourselves from the myth that the only and best way to raise a child depends on the presence of a man we call a father.

It's also a call to reexamine what we expect from fathers, present or not. What's imagined is Cliff Huxtable trading wit and canned wisdom with his children before traipsing off to a job that enables him to provide financially, then coming home to hand out a healthy dose of necessary discipline to keep the children well behaved. What's real is that having a father in the home increases the likelihood for abuse for both the spouse and children. What's real are fathers who are broken and showing up to fill a role that they themselves are struggling to understand. We have spent so much time valorizing the mere existence of fathers, we haven't discussed what type of fathers they will be. We haven't shown any concern for whether or not these fathers show up as full, healthy human beings.

To his credit, Obama addressed this in his Father's Day speech when he said: "[Children] see when you are ignoring or mistreating your wife. They see when you are inconsiderate at home; or when you are distant; or when you are thinking only of yourself. And so it's no surprise when we see that behavior in our schools or on our streets." Only, these are exactly the things we expect from fathers. We have never asked that they be nurturing and kind, loving and understanding, but simply present and providing. And then we want them to pass that down to the next generation.

When we say "a boy needs a father," we mean "a boy needs someone to teach him how to be a patriarch." Teach him to suppress, teach him to be unfeeling, teach him to lead without asking, teach him solitude, teach him not to cope, teach him to explode. All in the name of maintaining the myth.

Every lesson my father ever taught me came back to the myth. "One day, when you have a son of your own," he would say, "you'll understand." I have no son of my own, but I understand. I understand that my father carried the pain of feeling abandoned by his father, and vowed to not be like him. I understand that my father became the type of father he wished he had. I understand that for him a father was meant to set an example of hard work, that he should pass along valuable life lessons about handling money, that he should teach you how to drive and tie a double windsor, that he should come down hard when you lie or fail to live up to your potential.

I also understand that as a shy, insecure kid who wanted someone to talk to about his fears, there was a distance between me and my father. As someone who needed to know that I would be loved even through my mistakes, my father's raised eyebrows and voice and belt weren't reassuring. His way of buying affection without speaking through his feelings made it harder to get close. His cold reactions to some of my proudest moments didn't ease us toward embrace.

When I tell the story of my relationship with my father, the response I hear most often is, "You had it better than most. Be grateful he was there." And once again, the myth prevents us from seeing. I did have it better than most. I'll never deny that. My father's sacrifices meant that I never went homeless or hungry, unclothed or unwashed. Materially, I had all that I could ask for and more. He made that possible. I would not be writing these words today if he didn't. I'm grateful.

But it doesn't mean that the strain and tension between us didn't have an effect on me, on my sense of self. I didn't like myself for a long time, and much of that had to do with never feeling like I could do anything worthy enough to receive my father's love. Perfection, if I could achieve such a thing, felt inadequate. I know now that it isn't true, that he loved me in the way he knew how and that he always would, but that's not what shaped me. As I got older, watching him cling to his stoicism, never softening his edge, never opening up to his pain, made our relationship make sense but made me mourn for what could have been. Now, it isn't about me. I wish he could be there for himself.

And sometimes, he tried. Every once in a while you could see him trying to push past his own understanding of himself and his role as a father to be the kind of emotionally present man of my imagination. But no one ever asked him, "How did you learn to be a black man? How did you learn to be a black father?," and he never had to find an answer. He, like other black men, let the script guide him more often than not. Part of that script is producing memories through major milestones. So he woke me up at 4 a.m. on November 4, 2008, and we stood in line to make history.

In the years since, I've had to wonder if history was worth it. That speech at Apostolic Church of God wasn't a one-off. One of the frustrations of the Obama presidency is that only a figure like Barack Obama could become the first black president. He's black in a way that allows (not all, but enough) white people to be comfortable with America's history of racism. They can ignore it because Obama largely ignores it. They can celebrate progress because Obama celebrates and represents progress. And they can place some of the blame for the condition of black life in America on black folks because Obama, whenever speaking directly to black people, does the same thing.

I don't believe he has done so for the benefit of white people, but it certainly helped separate him from the traditional "race man" who could never have been elected president. But this is what he actually believes. He comes out of a school of thinking that may acknowledge the existence of racism, but sees it as the responsibility of black people to overcome, to achieve in the face of racism, not push for its end. In a way, it's a response to the late Derrick Bell's assertion that racism is a permanent fixture of American life. If racism is intractable, why waste energy fighting it, when you could be spending time doing the work of bettering yourself?

Of late, this school of thought has been called "politics of respectability." When historian Evelyn Brooks Higginbotham coined that term in her 1993 book *Righteous Discontent: The Women's Movement in the Black Baptist Church, 1880–1920*, that wasn't exactly what she meant by it. She was naming the philosophy of black church women at the turn of the twentieth century that "emphasized reform of individual behavior and attitudes both as a goal in itself and as a strategy for reform of the entire structural system of American race relations." The idea being that if black people were able to disprove the racist stereotypes of black inferiority by being citizens of the greatest moral regard, the institutions of racism would no longer have any basis for their standing. "Fight segregation through the courts as an unlawful act? Yes," a statement from the executive board of the Women's Convention states. "But fight it with soap and water, hoes, spades, shovels and paint to remove any reasonable excuse for it."

The most famous example of the application of this philosophy in black liberation activism is the Montgomery Bus Boycott. Rosa Parks became an emblem of injustice not only by virtue of her exemplary courage, but because it would have been more difficult to rally support behind Claudette Colvin, the unwed pregnant teenager arrested for refusing to give up her seat nine months before Parks. If part of the argument against racism were to rest on black people's moral authority, the fifteen-year-old Colvin couldn't become the face of the movement.

Noble as the intentions of respectability politics may have once been, it's a philosophy that has morphed over time into another tool to blame black people for their own oppression. What was a strategy of resistance became an admonishment toward conformity. Invoking the politics of respectability now is to name a more conservative strain of thought where it is believed that if you behave "properly," dress "well," speak "correctly," get the "right" education, and listen to authority, whatever racism that does exist in the world will not be an impediment to your success. If you adhere to the rules of society, your race will not matter. It's only when we live up to the stereotypes that we limit our opportunities.

This isn't just a diminishment of the impact of racism, but a misreading of how racism operates. There are no traits that are inherent to blackness that then become the basis for oppression. It's the other way around. The system of racism invented, and continually adjusts, the rubric to justify its existence. Whether we're talking about the idea that enslaved Africans were a less evolved form of the human species and therefore better suited to field work, on down to identifying who is and isn't a thug based on their fashion choices and patterns of speech, the underlying context is that black is other. Thug is black is nigger. America is nothing without its nigger.

In that regard, politics of respectability cedes the terms of respect to the white racist imagination. If we are starting from a moral standard that excludes blackness, in all its forms, it's one that we can never live up to. We can not achieve respect from the system because we've been defined out of it before we can finish our double windsors.

But if we look back to what politics of respectability was initially meant to describe, it's still an insufficient philosophy. Part of the reason why a new generation of thinkers and activists has rejected respectability politics is that it's by necessity a politics of exclusion. With the goal being to gain the respect of those in charge of maintaining an anti-black, anti-woman, anti-queer, anti-trans, anti-poor system, the field of who counts as "respectable" is so narrowed that who and what you organize doesn't make for an inclusive vision of freedom. Do sex workers count as respectable? Do drug dealers count? Do the incarcerated count? Do low-wage fast food workers count? Do single mothers count? Do high school dropouts count? And if they don't, what issues are our politics organizing around? What future are we envisioning?

Because we have witnessed the limitations of this thinking, this is what has brought us to our current moment. The more we center the most "respectable," the more people we make invisible; the more we celebrate representation, whether it's Obama or Idris Elba, without systemic change, the more deeply entrenched white supremacy becomes. We shouldn't be seeking the respect of an unjust system that will not respect us on the basis of our humanity alone. We cannot allow those terms to make the fight for justice mirror our broader system that relies on the oppression of the least "respectable." We must abandon the hierarchies. Our challenge is to take the spirit with which we have fought for black men—cisgender, heterosexual, class privileged, educated black men—and extend it to the fight for everyone else.

That's not to diminish what progress has been made through respectability politics. The victories of the Civil Rights movement are real and felt by us all. If all we want is progress, in its fits and starts and pushback and undoing, it's an argument worth considering. But a radical politics of liberation for all of us will look much different.

Because the election of President Obama was progress. There's no denying that. The ability of a nation founded on the enslavement of African people to elect a black man named Barack Hussein Obama to the highest office in the land is no small thing. It's representative of some shift. But by every measure, Obama also represents the most "respectable" black man this country has ever produced. And what has his respectability won him but disrespect?

He did everything. He studied hard. He went to Harvard. He got married. He had children. He worked. He dreamed big. He pulled his bootstraps all the way up from his humble beginnings to the presidency. He lived the American Dream. And he was called an African witch doctor. People asked for his birth certificate. A congressman shouted at him "YOU LIE!" He faced the most recalcitrant Republican Congress ever that was elected by a constituency that wanted to "take the country back." If a black man can be elected as guardian of the American empire, do exactly that, and still not be shielded from racism, what hope is supposed to be left?

It has been one of the more frustrating things to watch during the Obama presidency. He could see clearly what has happened to him, the most accomplished black politician ever, and know why, but still stand before a graduating class at Morehouse and talk about "excuses."

By May 2013, Obama's lectures to Black America had taken a backseat to his attempts at negotiating with Republicans, but he made his triumphant return in front of Morehouse College's Class of 2013. In all fairness to Obama, a college commencement address isn't the place for a detailed policy speech, but it also shouldn't be a place for this: "Nobody cares how tough your upbringing was. Nobody cares if you suffered some discrimination. And moreover, you have to remember that whatever you've gone through, it pales in comparison to the hardships previous generations endured—and they overcame them. And if they overcame them, you can overcome them, too." Because someone should care. And it would be nice if the president these young men were supposed to see themselves in cared. We make a grave mistake every time we invoke the history of oppression to diminish the reality of racism's present. Progress is real, but the narrative of progress seduces us into inaction. If we believe, simply, that it gets better, there is no incentive to do the work to ensure that it does.

That's something Obama knows, and acknowledged as much a few months later in his speech commemorating the fiftieth anniversary of the March on Washington for Jobs and Freedom. "We would dishonor those heroes as well to suggest that the work of this nation is somehow complete," he said. "The arc of the moral universe may bend towards justice, but it doesn't bend on its own. To secure the gains this country has made requires constant vigilance, not complacency."

Had he stopped there, he would have delivered a perfectly fitting speech for the occasion. But he couldn't resist that patented Obama evenhandedness, so he added:

> And then, if we're honest with ourselves, we'll admit that during the course of fifty years, there were times when some of us claiming to push for change lost our way. The anguish of assassinations set off self-defeating riots. Legitimate grievances against police brutality tipped into excuse-making for criminal behavior. Racial politics could cut both ways, as the transformative message of unity and brotherhood was drowned out by the language of recrimination. And what had once been a call for equality of opportunity, the chance for all Americans to work hard and get ahead was too often framed as a mere desire for government support—as if we had no agency in our own liberation, as if poverty was an excuse for not raising your child, and the bigotry of others was reason to give up on yourself.

As if "riots" were not a response to generations of poverty, state violence, and a nation looking away. As if "criminal behavior" hasn't been continually redefined to mean "anything a black person does." As if "unity," not freedom, has ever been the goal. As if working hard has ever been sufficient for any group of people in this country, and government support didn't create the white middle class that has been so fetishized. As if people haven't always done the best they can no matter their circumstance.

But it was a moment in between the Morehouse commencement and the March on Washington speech that led to my greatest frustration. When President Obama addressed the nation after George Zimmerman was acquitted for killing Trayvon Martin. When he said, "Trayvon Martin could have been me." When it felt like having a black president to explain our experience to the rest of the country could be transformational. When it seemed like he could finally see us.

A speech is a speech, though. His plan of action was not an agenda to decriminalize black life. It was a partnership between nonprofit organizations and corporations to provide increased mentorship for young black men, called My Brother's Keeper.

There is nothing wrong with promoting mentorship. There is something wrong with a president who told us for years that he was not the president of Black America but all of America, as if black people were not part of America, now putting forth his first racially specific program, and it not being any policy, but rather a spate of philanthropic endeavors. It was insulting, but right in line with his philosophy.

As if he had been elected to be mentor in chief. As if mentors are all black boys need to survive. As if what he really meant was mentor as a stand in for father. As if he could save black boys by becoming their surrogate father. As if we can afford to continue believing the myth.

Trayvon Martin had a father. Jordan Davis had a father. Michael Brown had a father. Tamir Rice had a father. Having a father won't protect black boys from America.

More frustrating is thinking that there was a time when I would have agreed with Obama. All of the people I looked to early on as teachers were influenced to some degree by respectability politics, and the narrative of the endangered black male, and the myth of patriarchy saving us. To be taken seriously as a black thinker, you had to balance your systemic analysis with large portions of black pathology. You couldn't critique police violence without adding contextless concerns about "black-on-black" gun violence. You couldn't decry the War on Drugs without also denigrating the drug dealers and the addicts. And I wanted to be a good black writer, so I did all of those things. I believed them.

I believed, on November 4, 2008, as CNN was calling the election and I'd finally gotten enough sleep to be coherent, that a new America was within our reach. Sitting there in front of the same television set that brought me Dave Chappelle sketches and LeBron James dunks, I saw a new history unfolding, one with hope at its center. "If there is anyone out there who still doubts that America is a place where all things are possible," I heard as I stared, "who still wonders if the dream of our founders is alive in our time," I heard as I held back tears, "who still questions the power of our democracy, tonight is your answer." President Barack Obama. A black man.

Born in 1986, raised on multiculturalism and diversity, a millennial in every sense, I was supposed to believe this was possible, but I didn't until it happened. I believed I would go to my grave having never seen a black president of the United States. I was proven wrong, and I wanted then to believe I would be wrong about so many things.

I wanted president-elect Barack Obama's words, "This is your victory," to be aimed directly at me, the unemployed college failure with an anxiety disorder who wanted to be an honest black man and a good black writer. I wanted my father's words, said in passing, "It's a new day," to be less of a platitude and more a declaration. I wanted my younger brother, sitting beside me and not yet old enough to vote, to believe, too. I was glad that, if I ever did have a child, I wouldn't have to tell them the same unintentional lie my parents told me. "You can be anything you want to be" was now true. I wanted that to mean free.

And then Oscar Grant was killed. On January 1, 2009, not even a full month after we elected the first black president of the United States, Officer Johannes Mehserle shot and killed twenty-two-year-old Oscar Grant in Oakland, California.

Mehserle and several other officers were responding to the report of a fight breaking out on the BART train. Oscar and his friends were identified among those involved. While the officers handcuffed some of the young men, they claim Oscar was resisting arrest. They attempted to restrain him, and in their attempts Mehserle claims to have reached for his Taser, but pulled out his gun instead. He fired a shot.

Oscar Grant's last words were, "You shot me! I got a daughter."

On July 8, 2010, the same day LeBron James announced he would take his talents to South Beach, Mehserle was convicted of involuntary manslaughter and was later sentenced to two years in prison, minus time served.

Before Eric Garner and Tamir Rice and Walter Scott, we saw Oscar Grant killed. The incident was captured on several cell phone cameras and the footage began circulating on social media almost immediately. I watched the video over and over again. I watched someone my age, born the same year that I was, someone else who was supposed to believe in the dawn of a new history, be shot in the back. I watched a father have his life taken.

For the first three years of Obama's presidency, every time he spoke I would think of Oscar. And how progress can produce amnesia. And how America periodically issues violent reminders that its niggers are still niggers. And how I wanted to believe. And how it was impossible to do so and become an honest black man and a good black writer.

And then George Zimmerman killed Trayvon Martin, and I asked myself, "How did you learn to be a black man?" And I didn't have an answer. And I went searching my life and the lives of those around me to find one. And I found not one, but many. And they didn't all make sense. And they didn't all make me feel better. And yet I couldn't look away.

And then I wrote furious, sobering words to try and help me understand. And maybe help someone else understand, too. And they never felt like enough. And they still don't.

And then Michael Brown. And then Freddie Gray. And then the fire came and the nation didn't know what to do with it. And Obama couldn't save them. And we picked up the bricks because the ballots weren't strong enough. And the glass broke the same way our bodies did. And they finally saw us.

And as the rest of the world watches, we still try to learn how to see ourselves.

Conclusion

I am twenty-nine years old now. It's not unheard of; the actual life expectancy for black men in America is seventy-two. But it still feels like I'm not supposed to be here.

I wasn't supposed to go to college or write a book. I wasn't supposed to vote for the first black president or drop out of college. I wasn't supposed to fall in love or reevaluate my relationship to weed. I wasn't supposed to buy more sneakers than I can count or run from police in Ferguson. Or feel guilty about it all.

I still think about Trayvon. And Oscar. And Sean. And Jordan. And Ramarley. And Tamir. And Michael. And Freddie. I still think about what they won't have the opportunity to do. They're not here to give their opinion on the latest Kendrick Lamar record, or get drunk at Howard's homecoming, or imitate Stephen Curry's jump shot, or demand more from Obama's successor.

Dwelling on that guilt, though, isn't productive. I'm here. I'm a black boy who became a black man in America. And I got the chance to ask myself what that means.

It's a process of self-creation in a society that has already defined you. It's resisting that definition because it denies your humanity. It's fighting to live long enough to recognize your own humanity. It's fighting for the freedom to define yourself on your own terms.

It's learning that freedom comes with responsibility. It's learning to bend in the places where your self-definition begins to deny others the freedom to define themselves. It's letting go of the old ideas that helped you survive and embracing new ones to help you, and everyone around you, thrive.

It's recognizing that the process is never complete. It's knowing the fight won't be easy but will be worth it. It's reminding yourself of that when it would be much easier to give up. It's wanting to give up every day. It's loving yourself enough not to.

It's knowing that there will always be more questions. It's realizing that the answer to "How did you learn to be a black man?" will change. I'm twenty-nine years old now, and I'm different than I was when I was seventeen. I created a self in response to the way the world shifted when I thought I wasn't supposed to be here. I changed as the politics, culture, movements, symbols, and martyrs changed.

There are more symbols and martyrs now. There will, unfortunately, be more later. Some of them will look like Trayvon, others like Sandra Bland, still others like Ty Underwood and

Penny Proud. They will make us ask more questions of ourselves. Hopefully our answers to those questions will make us more free. Hopefully our answers will produce fewer martyrs.

But we have to start with the right questions. We re-create white supremacy, misogyny, homophobia, transphobia, class-based elitism, self-hatred, violence, and untreated mental illness in part because we have failed to ask the right questions about how to end them. So far we've mostly asked how we can stop the bleeding.

I started this book with the question, "How did you learn to be a black man?" I thought understanding how I became who I am would help me better understand who I want to be. Examining my influences, both powerful and mundane, and the lessons from the most meaningful people and events of my life was meant to draw a sketch of the black man I've become.

The answers I came up with here are what's true for me now. If I'm lucky, I'll get to answer the question again when I'm thirty-nine, forty-nine, fifty-nine, and beyond.

Or I'll realize that it wasn't the right question. And then I'll start with a new one. There will always be more questions. The right ones can only be found through trial and error.

I hope I stumbled upon a useful question here. I hope this serves something greater than my own understanding of myself. I hope I created a self that helps others thrive. I hope my answers create a world where the Trayvons in waiting can see their own humanity. I hope I've fought hard enough to live long enough to see what questions they ask.

I hope their answers are better than mine.

ACKNOWLEDGMENTS

And this is for . . .

My family: my Gail, Daddy, Jerel, dear sweet Auntie Gay, Antaeus, Darius, Marcus, Granny, Uncle Al, Jeffrey Severe.

My co-conspirators, without whom this book wouldn't have been written: Katy O'Donnell, Jessica Papin, Alessandra Bastagli.

My friends, colleagues, and comrades whose contributions to and support of this project are worth more than their brief acknowledgment here: Bassey Ikpi, Marc Lamont Hill, Kiese Laymon, R. L'Heureux Lewis-McCoy, Mark Anthony Neal, Darnell L. Moore, Marlon Peterson, Kai M. Green, Hashim Pipkin, Wade Davis, Nyle Fort, Salamishah Tillet, Tayari Jones, Jessica Valenti, Lori Adelman, Josie Duffy, Joan Morgan, Brittney Cooper, Treva Lindsey, Kimberlé Crenshaw, Ava DuVernay, Melissa Harris-Perry, Janet Mock, Charlene Carruthers, Dante Barry, umi selah, Alicia Garza, Tory Russell, Jamilah Lemieux, Alencia Johnson, Jessica Byrd, Jermaine Spradley, Tall Ass Ian Blair,

Kiara Pesante Haughton, Ruby-Beth Buitekant, Tiq Milan, Ryan Devereaux, Abby Ellis, Sarah Leonard, Jesse Myerson, Molly Knefel, John Knefel, Meredith Clark, Gideon Oliver, Natasha Lennard, Lukas Hermsmeier, Josh Begley, Nick Pinto, Kristen Gwynne, Ali Gharib, Alyona Minkovski, Andrea Jones, Melissa Gira Grant, Tommy Moore, Ned Resnikoff, Cora Currier, Rembert Browne, Syreeta McFadden, Alana Massey, Amy Rose Spiegel, Annie Shields, Frank Reynolds, Kate Murphy, Caitlin Graf, Liliana Segura, Maya Dusenbery, Chloe Angyal, Alexandra Brodsky, Vanessa Valenti, Samhita Mukhopadhyay, Taya Kitman, Annelise Whitley, Roz Hunter, Katrina vanden Heuvel, Emily Douglas, Kai Wright, Richard Kim, and everyone I'm sure I missed but swear I didn't mean anything by it.

My soundtracks: *Black on Both Sides*, *The Blueprint*, *Lord Willin'*, *The College Dropout*, *Thug Motivation 101*, *good kid, m.A.A.d. city*, *Run the Jewels 2*.

Everyone whose text I never returned, email I neglected, date I cancelled in order to get this done. Hope you understand.

Stacy, Anna, Nora, and everyone else at Café Ghia.

The Teenage Mutant Ninja Turtles.

Demetri.

You, for buying the book and taking the time to read it. Truly, thanks for **BUYING** the book and taking the time to **READ** it.

The martyrs, the tokens, and the movement.

CREDITS

Mychal Denzel Smith is a Knobler Fellow at the Nation Institute and a contributing writer for the *Nation* magazine. He has also written for the *New York Times*, *Atlantic*, *Salon*, Feministing.com, *Guardian*, *Root*, *theGrio*, *ThinkProgress*, and *Huffington Post*, and he has been a featured commentator on NPR, BBC radio, CNN, MSNBC, Al Jazeera America, HuffPost Live, and a number of other radio and television programs. Follow him @mychalsmith.

**NATION
BOOKS**

The Nation Institute

Nation.

Founded in 2000, **Nation Books** has become a leading voice in American independent publishing. The inspiration for the imprint came from the *Nation* magazine, the oldest independent and continuously published weekly magazine of politics and culture in the United States.

The imprint's mission is to produce authoritative books that break new ground and shed light on current social and political issues. We publish established authors who are leaders in their area of expertise, and endeavor to cultivate a new generation of emerging and talented writers. With each of our books we aim to positively affect cultural and political discourse.

Nation Books is a project of The Nation Institute, a nonprofit media center established to extend the reach of democratic ideals and strengthen the independent press. The Nation Institute is home to a dynamic range of programs: our award-winning Investigative Fund, which supports ground-breaking investigative journalism; the widely read and syndicated website TomDispatch; our internship program in conjunction with the *Nation* magazine; and Journalism Fellowships that fund up to 20 high-profile reporters every year.

For more information on Nation Books, the *Nation* magazine, and The Nation Institute, please visit:

www.nationbooks.org
www.nationinstitute.org
www.thenation.com
www.facebook.com/nationbooks.ny
Twitter: @nationbooks